The Abolition of God

HANS-GERHARD KOCH

The Abolition of God

Materialistic Atheism and
Christian Religion

FORTRESS PRESS

PHILADELPHIA

Translated by Robert W. Fenn from the German
*Abschaffung Gottes? Der materialistische Atheismus
als heutige Existenzform*,
Stuttgart, Quell-Verlag der evang. Gesellschaft, 1961

Library of Congress Catalog Card Number: 63–13877

FIRST PUBLISHED 1963
© SCM PRESS LTD 1963
PRINTED IN GREAT BRITAIN

Contents

Translator's Note

'HOW CAN GOD BE REAL, IF HE IS NOT MATERIAL ?' IN HIS
book *A Christian in East Germany* (SCM Press, London, and
Association Press, New York), Pastor Johannes Hamel records
being asked this question during one of his many conversations
with Marxists. The present book seems to be the fullest answer
to this typical protest.

The book derives from the author's long and intimate contact
with the crass materialistic form of atheism dominant in the Soviet
Union and the East German Republic. Dr Koch was a prisoner of
war in Russian hands from 1945 until he took up pastoral work in
Halle in the East German Republic (DDR) in 1950. As a minister
and as the father of three children, he was alarmed at the pressure
of anti-Christian propaganda in the schools, press and radio. This
and the recurrent necessity of meeting seriously the criticism
advanced by his communist friends against the Church and the
Christian way of life drove him to an intensive study of the communist ideology and its impact on the lives of the Russian and East
German people. He realized that materialistic atheism must be
taken seriously. Uninformed and superficial repudiation was not
enough. Effective criticism of Marxist atheism from the Christian
standpoint could only be made from the fullest knowledge. Only
through a clear mutual understanding of the fundamental beliefs
of both sides could any vital contact be made and the Christian
Gospel presented in its real relevance. That is what this book is
about. Dr Koch published it after moving to an academic position
in West Germany in 1960.

Two points should be noted by the reader. The word *evangelisch* (which has usually been translated 'evangelical') simply means 'Protestant' as over against 'Roman Catholic'; it does not refer to 'low-church' as over against 'high-church' as is frequently the case in English usage. Also, because of his personal experience and because of recent German history and custom, the author uses the term 'socialist' interchangeably with the term 'communist' rather than distinguishing the terms as is commonly done in the English-speaking world.

ROBERT W. FENN

The Abolition of God

Preface

THE CRITICAL EXAMINATION OF THE CONFLICT BETWEEN evangelical faith and materialistic atheism attempted in this volume follows the New Testament injunction binding on all of us who call ourselves Christians: 'Always be prepared to make a defence to any one who calls you to account for the hope that is in you' (I Peter 3.15).

The need for such an analysis is incontestable. Christ himself claims to be the Way, the Truth and the Life, even for those who have turned away from him. Atheism and its adherents are still part of God's world and are included in his love.

Most of the assertions about the Christian faith made by materialistic atheism so far have been confined to mere polemics, and are too superficial to lead to any serious discussion. On the other hand the evangelical Church has so far failed to recognize either the necessity for or the advantage in such a comprehensive discussion, and instead has confined itself to a few isolated statements and some preliminary study.

The difficulty is that both the evangelical faith and materialistic atheism are complex structures offering the possibility of confrontation at many different levels. Furthermore the non-Marxist reader finds his approach to the literature and the method of argument of materialistic atheism made more difficult by a wide divergence of terminology and logic.

The initial task of any analysis therefore is to sort out and arrange the material and to establish the vital points of difference so that the real problem may become clear and can be systematically discussed. To this end the present inquiry has been confined to the foremost representatives and profoundest interpreters of materialistic atheism. It is expected to lead to the consideration of the fundamental questions at issue between evangelical faith and materialistic atheism.

To identify the evangelical standpoint with the West and the atheistic with the East is much too facile. The problem goes far deeper and cuts right across the division of the world into two groups—indeed it directly affects each individual. Hence the purpose of this inquiry is simply to serve the cause of truth and justice.

The prospect of any successful outcome of this discussion is not particularly bright, but that is no reason to abandon it. The important thing is to attempt a first step towards understanding and to work out a genuine evangelical answer.

The book is not intended as a vindication, still less as an apologia, but a discussion with the mind kept open to the arguments of the other side. It aims at providing an answer for those who are perplexed and have renounced their faith, and also for those who feel satisfied with their position.

The most important task therefore will be to get down to the basic questions involved in materialistic atheism. Only when the Christian understands these questions in their full dimensions can he venture to offer an answer from the truth of the Gospel, the illumination of faith and the power of love. Only when a question has been understood and has become a challenge, is it possible to start looking for an answer.

Since materialistic atheism makes an unqualified judgment on the basis of a caricature of the Christian faith and thus misses the truth of God and salvation, and since Christians often fail to recognize the questions underlying materialistic atheism and so make premature judgments about it, the following exposition seeks to make a contribution towards a real relaxation of tension in the intellectual field. There is urgent need for this today.

Introduction

THE BASIS OF THE EVANGELICAL FAITH IS GOD'S revelation in Christ and the acceptance of his offer of salvation. Consequently it is 'erroneous doctrine to maintain that there are areas of our life in which we owe allegiance to other masters than Jesus Christ, areas where we do not need his justification and sanctification' (Barmen Declaration, Thesis 2).

Materialistic atheism on the other hand is based on a view of the world in which either matter or dialectics is the ultimate ground of being, a view that is essentially atheistic.

Thus evangelical faith and materialistic atheism stand diametrically opposed, as two fundamentally different views of the world with corresponding assumptions about reality. A greater contrast is neither possible nor conceivable and they represent opposite poles in the history of western thought.

In so far as both systems offer definite views about the world and man's place in it, they come into conflict in the most diverse places. There is hardly any department of human life and culture that is unaffected by both systems, and which does not therefore become a scene of conflict. Hence the surprising fact emerges that evangelical faith and materialistic atheism have much more in common in regard to the scope of their immediate concerns than might be at first supposed. In its modern theology the evangelical faith is forced to face frankly the problems of human existence, while materialistic atheism also has examined all the human problems, sciences and forms of culture within its range of view in order to find a 'scientific' answer. It is from such observations and considerations that the argument of this book has been developed.

The first part inquires what materialistic atheism with its view of the historical development of human thought has to say, and describes how it tries to understand the phenomenon of religion, what attitude it takes to the Bible, and what it says about the Christian faith and about Christ himself.

These four aspects of materialistic atheism, which are of concern to the Christian faith, are then subjected to a critical examination which could well provide a basis for discussion.

In this first primarily expository section the main concern is to set out factually the statements of atheistic belief that are of decisive importance for evangelical faith.

The second part attempts to give an answer to the questions raised by materialistic atheism, an answer that is not only a refutation of its fundamental godlessness, but also has regard to those features of atheism that make it a cathartic and purifying agent for evangelical faith.

This consideration of the basis of materialistic atheism shows it not only in its actual revolt against God, but also in its serious protest against the short-comings of the Church and of Christendom. Here the Church has to accept some criticism from materialistic atheism, but it has also something to say in return. Ultimately the living Christian faith confronts atheism with the reality and truth of God, but it has also this criticism to make, that atheism has not really solved the question of the existence of God, either from the outmoded position of Feuerbach or from more modern philosophical considerations, but that in fact the question still remains to be faced.

In the middle of the twentieth century for a variety of reasons questions concerning faith and the Church have become so much more acute that Christians have to face rigorous catechism from the world, and so also from materialistic atheism. The result has been the discarding of supports that have become rotten—like basing Christian faith on emotion or on any human agency, and the questionable help from non-evangelical sources—in order that the Gospel of Christ may shine forth more brightly and be more effective.

Evangelical faith leaves room to take materialistic atheism very seriously and forbids any superficial judgment on mere prejudice, but looks at things at many levels and in their full depth, so that a definitely positive judgment can be made.

The final conclusion is that the God and Father of our Lord Jesus Christ testified to in the Bible is unaffected by any argumentation on the part of materialistic atheism. Therefore, the Christian cannot give up his faith in God and Christ, but must confess it and maintain its truth, not in order to annoy or shame any individual atheist, but in order to confront him with the ultimate and profound truth, that means salvation for all men and the true peace of the world.

I · Materialistic Atheism on Religion and Christianity

1 · The Atheistic Tradition

IN THE WEST THERE HAS EXISTED FOR CENTURIES AN unbroken Christian tradition represented by such outstanding names as Paul, Augustine and Luther. Materialistic atheism also has discovered in history a tradition of its own, that stands in opposition to the Christian and idealistic one. It was Karl Marx who took the first step in this process, when he hailed the Greek hero Prometheus as 'the most distinguished saint and martyr in the philosophic calendar'.[1] By that he meant that materialistic atheism did not regard itself as a new phenomenon beginning in the nineteenth century, but as a philosophy that had absorbed from human history all that it considered 'positive' and had developed it under the slogan of 'progress'. Thus an account of the atheistic tradition must not be confined to the rise of modern materialistic atheism, but it must also inquire into its fundamental criteria and principles of evaluation. The materialistic atheistic tradition has so far received little attention from Christianity, although materialistic atheism has clearly derived all its essential elements from it. The first volume of a four-volume History of Philosophy, published in 1959 and written from the materialistic-atheistic point of view, together with one or two earlier publications, provide material for this description of the atheistic tradition.

Principles of Evaluation

Materialistic atheism has searched carefully through the history of the nations from the earliest times for indications of atheistic

[1] Marx-Engels, *On Religion* (Foreign Languages Publishing House, Moscow) [1957], p. 15.

thinking, and has in fact brought to light a few insignificant traces of anti-religious ideas. Marx and Engels, both well read in the history of philosophy, discovered germs of atheistic ideas in the beginning of scientific thinking amongst the ancient Greeks. Here they made their principle of selection, criterion and pattern the distinction between idealism and materialism.

Friedrich Engels (1820-1895) derived the criterion materialism/ idealism from what he regarded as the most important question of philosophy, the relation between thinking and being, and he reduced it to the concise formula: Idealism means the primacy of mind over nature and thus in the end implies the creation of the world. Materialism on the other hand regards nature as primary and maintains that the world has existed always.[1]

It was from this challenging antithesis—the world as creation or as always existing—that Engels derived his principle of selection, criterion and pattern. His standard of evaluation thus becomes basically a theological matter, because beneath the philosophical trappings it is ultimately concerned with God. Wherever in any system of thought there is assumed to be no place for God, e.g. in materialism, Engels uses positive terms like 'valuable', 'useful', 'progressive', but where in his opinion there is still room for belief in God, e.g. in idealism, he uses negative assessments like 'retrograde', 'oppressive', 'unscientific'.

Zhdanov was completely in line with Engels' thought in his definition of the atheistic criterion for history, when he said in 1947 that the scientific history of philosophy was essentially the history of the inception, rise and development of materialist ideology and its laws.[2]

In ancient history, however, the types in the materialism/ idealism pattern are never quite pure, but are obscured in complicated hybrid forms. For example, Democritus is judged inconsistently. Philosophically he is accepted as a progressive materialist but politically he is rejected as an ideologist of the slave-owners. Nevertheless the pattern serves as a guide by which

---

[1] Engels, *Ludwig Feuerbach* (ET ed. C. P. Dutt), London 1934, p. 31.

[2] A. A. Zhdanov, *Kritische Bemerkungen zu G. F. Alexandrows Buch 'Gesch. der westeur. Philosophie'*, Berlin 1950, p. 6.

materialistic atheism can find its way through the confused story of man's intellectual development and can arrive at value judgments.

The Archetype

In his dissertation for the doctorate (Jena, 1841) entitled 'Comparison of the Natural Philosophy of Democritus and Epicurus' Karl Marx provided the stimulus for the development of a materialistic-atheistic tradition by setting up the titanic figure of Prometheus as the archetype. Prometheus became the archetype and pattern of defiance of the envy of the gods by his theft of fire from heaven in order to use it on earth in the interest of human life and culture. As punishment for his deed, according to Greek legend, Zeus chained him to a rock, where in the daytime an eagle devoured his liver, which, however, always grew again during the night.

When the twenty-three-year-old Marx called Prometheus 'the most distinguished saint and martyr in the philosophic calendar', he had in mind a philosophy with the basic creed: 'I hate the gods, who repay me with evil for the good I have done to them.'[1] According to Marx, Prometheus is opposed to 'all gods in earth or heaven that do not recognize man's self-consciousness as supreme. There shall be no other god but this.'[2] Marx' philosophic calendar therefore contains such 'saints and martyrs' as hate the gods and extol man's self-consciousness as the highest divinity. Prometheus thus becomes the representative of a view of man and the world that sets up his own self-consciousness as the ultimate reality and supreme good. Here atheism becomes the real underlying principle of philosophy generally.

In much the same way materialistic atheism found inspiration in Goethe's early poem *Prometheus*. The book *Universe, Earth and Man* (*Weltall, Erde und Mensch*) published in 1954 underlines Prometheus' scorn of the gods and extols the authoritarian idea of man formed in his own image.[3] Another book, distributed in 1957 at the Festival of Youth, *Our Germany* (*Unser Deutschland*) goes so far as to refer to Goethe's *Prometheus* as 'the poetical

---

[1] Marx-Engels, *On Religion*, p. 15, quoting Aeschylus' *Prometheus Bound.*
[2] *Ibid.*   [3] *Weltall, Erde und Mensch*, 1954, p. 9.

manifesto of German enlightenment' and maintains that Prometheus owed his splendour and pride neither to a superior authority nor to heaven, and that men should renounce their childish belief in a personal all-powerful God. Prometheus asserted that the generation he created after his own image would no longer bother about gods. By implication the Greek gods meant the Christian God also.[1] Marx' statement and the above quotation from 1957 are philosophically in line and contain a programme of atheistic world order and education.

Prometheus and his spirit are interpreted by modern theoretical atheism individually. In *O World in Light* (*Du Welt im Licht*) Stalin is likened to the ancient hero Prometheus, who brought fire and warmth and light to men, and whom no earthly power could shackle.[2] Here the Prometheus myth is transferred to a historical figure, obviously in praise of him.

In the official oration delivered at a festival in the Friedrich Schiller University at Jena in October 1957, the same university where 116 years earlier Karl Marx had submitted his dissertation for the doctorate with its apotheosis of Prometheus, these words, entirely in the Marxist spirit, were used: 'The great socialist October revolution in 1917 marked the hour when Prometheus man was freed for ever from the fetters with which philistinism had bound him. It was the hour of liberation for the Prometheus spirit, the hour of emancipation of science. It represents the greatest triumph so far of scientific thinking in control of the historic process. For the first time in human history the process of social development was directed by a voluntary and permanent association of resolute men, who accepted solely the scientific criterion for their political actions.'[3]

Prometheus, the saint and martyr in the philosophic calendar, and still the pattern and ideal of materialistic atheism, is the symbol of the materialistic-atheistic tradition as opposed to the Jewish-Christian. The contrast between Promethean and Christian man is the main issue in the conflict between evangelical faith and materialistic atheism.

[1] *Unser Deutschland*, p. 129.   [2] *Du Welt im Licht*, Berlin 1954, p. 14.
[3] Wilhelm Girnus, *Die Befreiung des prometheischen Menschen*, Address to the University of Jena, October 1957.

Atheism in Ancient Greece and Rome

Applying the pattern materialism/idealism to the philosophy of ancient Greece reveals two corresponding lines of thought. Modern atheism of course emphasises uncompromisingly the development of the materialistic tradition.

From the early period of Greek philosophy Thales of Miletus (*c.* 624-547 BC), Anaximander (*c.* 610-546) and Anaximenes (*c.* 585-526) are cited as materialists and praised as the founders of systematic Greek science. Indeed the whole of Greek philosophy is claimed by modern atheism: 'In antiquity atheism attained its highest development in the philosophy of ancient Greece under the progressive ideologists of the slave-owning democracy.' The materialistic Greek philosophers were held to have formulated for the first time the idea of the permanence of matter without the need of a creator. This contention is supported by reference to Parmenides, Heraclitus, Xenophon, Antiphon and Critias: 'Classical atheism manifests its most complete form in the systems of the materialistic philosophers Democritus, Epicurus and Lucretius Carus.' Democritus and Epicurus are held to have been the greatest scholars of antiquity.[1]

Heraclitus (*c.* 530-470) enjoys the greatest esteem in modern materialistic atheism, not as the result of any attempt at collating the surviving fragments of his writings, but because of a single idea of the Ephesian philosopher, which achieved a certain reputation in dialectical materialism. He said: 'The world was not made by gods or men, but it was and is and will be ever-living fire, self-igniting and self-extinguishing, according to measure or law.' Lenin's comment, with which Stalin agreed, was: 'A very good statement of the principles of dialectical materialism.'[2] This saying of Heraclitus is interpreted as meaning that the world did not have a creator, and is therefore regarded as being atheistic in spirit. Alongside Heraclitus, however, Leucippus and Democritus are also highly esteemed by modern materialistic atheism. Democritus

---

[1] F. N. Oleshchuk, *Atheismus* (Grosse Sowjet-Enzyklopädie: GSE), Berlin 1955, p. 4.

[2] V. I. Lenin, *Aus dem philos. Nachlass*, Berlin 1954, p. 276; J. Stalin, *Dialectical and Historical Materialism* (Little Stalin Library, No. 4), London 1941, p. 12.

(*c.* 460-370), the greatest materialist of antiquity, was held to have tried to explain the phenomena of nature scientifically, and to have destroyed belief in a hereafter and in the immortality of the soul. In contrast to Heraclitus and the materialists the great idealistic philosophers of ancient Greece, Socrates (469-399) and Plato (427-347) are condemned by modern materialistic atheism because their idealism is held to express the class interests of the reactionary slave-owners. About Aristotle (384-322) the verdict of modern athesim is not unanimous. On the one hand he is recognized as the greatest thinker of antiquity, but on the other hand it is maintained that his vacillation between the materialistic line of Democritus and the idealistic line of Plato makes him also responsible for introducing reactionary ideas.

Epicurus (341-270), on the contrary, as an advocate of atomic materialism wins approval even from Karl Marx, who called him the greatest Greek apostle of enlightenment, because he opposed superstition, mysticism and religion. Epicurus represented a further advance of Greek materialism, he said, by establishing the position of science in the struggle against the reactionary idea of a supernatural divine power. 'His physical-cosmological doctrine, that emphasises the eternity and permanence of the universe, was the crown of Greek science.'[1]

So much for the verdict of modern materialistic atheism on some of the ancient Greek philosophers.

Materialistic atheism, however, does not confine itself to the classification of well-known names and the atheistic interpretation of their individual sayings. It even hunts out long-forgotten names and ideas in support of its atheistic tradition.

The Great Soviet Encyclopaedia writes in this way about less-known but specifically atheistic thinkers of ancient Greece: 'In the conflict of materialism against idealism and religion Theodorus (end of the fourth century) played a significant part. He contested the existence of a god of any sort. Another atheistic thinker, Euhemeros (end of the fourth century and beginning of the third) the author of an attack on religion, *The Sacred History*, taught that the revered gods had been only men of

---

[1] *Das alte Griechenland* (GSE), Berlin 1954, p. 60.

earlier days distinguished for strength and intellect, rulers who had themselves introduced the cult of the worship of themselves.'[1]

Recently a third atheistic philosopher of ancient Greece has been unearthed, namely Diagoras the Atheist. Felix Jacoby in a philosophically unexceptionable monograph has collected all available data about Diagoras, but is unable to recognize him either as a creative thinker or a great philosopher, not even as a school philosopher. Nevertheless, Diagoras is said to have been the first philosopher to develop a clear and intelligible argument against the idea of God. He denied the possibility of the existence of any god or gods. His polemical book *Apopyrgizontes Logoi* ranked him as a hero in the fight against religion. [2]

It is a fundamental tendency of materialistic atheism unduly to exalt minor figures like Theodorus, Euhemerus and Diagoras, while important movements like Stoicism, Scepticism and Neo-Platonism are disproportionately belittled. All in all the specifically atheistic tradition of ancient Greek philosophy is without great historical importance or any real significance for the development of scientific thinking. The same is true of the atheistic tradition in the history of Roman philosophy, intellectual life and literature.

From the Roman period only one name need be mentioned as being overstressed by modern materialistic atheism, as far as his anti-religious importance is concerned: Lucretius Carus (96-55). Karl Marx called him 'a bold, lively, poetic master' and considered his didactic poem 'On the Nature of Things' to be one of the greatest works in world literature.[3] In this work Lucretius, a passionate poet and materialistic philosopher, expounds the doctrine of Epicurus as helping men towards happiness by freeing them from superstition. Actually this didactic poem does contain some elements of materialistic-atheistic ideas, such as the assertion of an ever-living nature, the permanence of matter, the denial of the immortality of the soul and a general tendency to optimism. Nevertheless, Lucretius too has his roots in mythology.

---

[1] *Ibid.*   [2] F. Jacoby, *Diagoras ho Atheos*, Berlin 1959.
[3] N. A. Mashkin, *Römische Geschichte*, Berlin 1953, p. 390.

Atheistic Tendencies in Medieval Arab-Jewish Philosophy

In the first few centuries AD the materialistic-atheistic tradition
was lost, but recently efforts have been made to find elements of
materialistic-atheistic thinking in the Arab-Jewish philosophers
of the eleventh and twelfth centuries.

Avicenna, doctor and philosopher from Tadshikistan, (Arabic,
Ibn Sina, 980-1037), Averroes, Spanish philosopher (Arabic,
Ibn Roschd, 1126-1198) and Maimonides, doctor and philosopher
in Spain, North Africa and Egypt (Rabbi Moses ben Maimon,
1135-1204), were all of considerable importance for the West,
because they conserved the legacy of Aristotle, so that medieval
scholasticism (Thomas Aquinas, Albertus Magnus and others)
could carry it further. Present-day materialistic-atheistic philosophers give Avicenna a place in the story of the development of
materialism from Aristotle up to Marx and Engels. Through
Avicenna, it was claimed, the divine index has been raised to the
higher power of matter. Avicenna's pantheism was regarded as
progressive for his time rather than retrograde. 'In the guise of
pantheism, which eliminates every outside supernatural power
and regards animate matter as primary, materialism appears
repeatedly in the Middle Ages and later. Pantheism is the expression of resistance against the feudal view of the world. God is
brought into the world and made part of nature. God is matter
and matter becomes God. This clearly points to atheism, and is a
declaration of war against supernatural mysticism.'[1]

It may be questioned whether the real essence of pantheism
has here been understood: what is certain is that it has been
interpreted in this atheistic sense by modern materialistic atheism
and made part of the atheistic tradition. That becomes more
evident in a comprehensive work by Hermann Ley, *Studies in the
History of Materialism in the Middle Ages* (*Studie zur Geschichte
des Materialismus in Mittelalter*). He is concerned here with the
continuous development of materialistic philosophy in the West,
particularly in the Saracen period. Avicenna, Averroes and others
are held to have introduced elements of materialism into their

[1] Heinrich Simon, 'Deutsche Beiträge zum Avicenna-Gedenkjahr 1952',
Deutsche Zeitschrift für Philosophie, 1953/2/415.

teaching and to have got very close to overt atheism: 'Notions like the doctrine of the eternity of matter, the unity of matter and motion, the creative power of matter, and the absorption of the individual consciousness in the whole, and also the concept of the active intellect, were particularly significant for further development.'[1] Ley maintains that each of these theses contradicts dogmatic theology and that this philosophy rejects in principle any form of creation story or that natural law can be violated by miracles, and denies categorically the assertion that the soul is immortal.[2]

Hermann Ley examined the history of medieval dogma for traces of atheism. His researches led him to the conclusion that 'it was not the official systems of Albertus and Thomas that were the real expression of the times, but their heretical opponents.'[3]

The Renaissance ushers in the Dawn of Enlightenment

In the view of materialistic atheism the Renaissance also forms part of the atheistic tradition. Marx and Engels had already emphasized its importance.

Engels' assessment of the Renaissance is well known: 'The spiritual domination of the Church was broken. . . . The Renaissance was the greatest progressive revolution that humanity had so far experienced, a time that needed giants and which produced giants—giants of intellect, passion and character, versatility and scholarship.'[4]

One reason for the high estimation of the Renaissance by materialistic atheism was the 'liberation of man from the yoke of the medieval Church' that it was supposed to have brought about: 'The authorities, traditions and dogmas that inhibited the free development of human thought in the Middle Ages, and on which the medieval scholastic theology rested, were subjected to critical examination.'[5]

According to Engels the Renaissance had ended a millennium of intellectual subjugation by the Church.

[1] H. Ley, *Studie zur Geschichte des Materialismus im Mittelalter*, p. 7.

[2] *Ibid.*   [3] *Op. cit.*, p. 509.

[4] Engels, *Dialectics of Nature* (Foreign Languages Publishing House, Moscow 1954), p. 30.

[5] *Die Renaissance* (GSE), Berlin 1954, p. 18.

Admittedly materialistic atheism sees the other side also, i.e. that the Renaissance enormously increased the exploitation of man by man, but that does not prevent materialistic atheism from drawing a very positive conclusion. Engels wrote: 'The achievement of the Renaissance, in spite of all the limitations resulting from the existing social conditions, was to lead men out of the darkness of the Middle Ages dominated by superstition into the dawn of an enlightened world of awakened minds.'[1]

Thus modern materialistic atheism regards the Renaissance as an important step on the way from a god-bound world into an enlightened godless world, and so as a milestone on the road of human progress.

Why Münzer and not Luther?

In the Reformation period modern atheism finds a representative of its tradition in Thomas Münzer, and contrasts him with Martin Luther, not only because of Luther's portentous attitude to the Peasants' Revolt, but also on account of his general views.

Friedrich Engels in his pamphlet *The Peasant War in Germany* (*Der deutsche Bauernkrieg*) has worked out the 'progressive' atheistic elements in Münzer's teaching, as the result of which he ranks him unquestionably higher than Luther, whom he describes as 'a lickspittle of the absolute monarchy' on account of his 'composition of a blatant dithyramb on divinely appointed authority.' In Engels' view Münzer's teaching is basically atheistic.

Engels' opinion has acquired considerable importance, because Münzer's account of Christianity is still accepted by modern materialistic atheism and has received official recognition.

About Münzer's teaching Engels writes: 'His theological-philosophical doctrine attacked all the main tenets not only of Catholicism but of Christianity in general. Within the general pattern of Christianity he taught a sort of pantheism that bears a remarkable resemblance to the modern speculative outlook, and in places comes close to atheism. He rejected the Bible as an exclusive or infallible revelation. The real and living revelation was reason, a revelation that has existed at all times among all peoples, and

[1] *Die Renaissance* (GSE), Berlin 1954, p. 18.

still exists. To set the Bible against reason was to kill the spirit with the letter, for the Holy Spirit of which the Bible speaks was nothing outside us. The Holy Spirit was reason. Faith was no more than the coming to life of reason, and so could be found also amongst the heathen. Through this faith, through reason becoming alive, men became godlike and happy. Heaven therefore was not to be thought of as beyond the grave: it was to be found in this life, and the duty of believers was to establish this heaven, the Kingdom of God, here on earth. Just as there was no heaven hereafter, so there was no future hell or damnation, nor was there any devil other than the evil desires and lusts of men. Christ was just a man like ourselves, a prophet and teacher, and the Lord's Supper was no more than a memorial meal, at which the bread and wine were taken without any mystical implications.'

Engels sums this up: 'Just as Münzer's religious philosophy comes close to atheism, so his political programme is not far short of communism.'[1] As a matter of fact Engels' presentation of Münzer's doctrine is not based on his own researches but on a book by Wilhelm Zimmermann *The Great German Peasants' Revolt (Der grosse deutsche Bauernkrieg).*[2]

Alfred Meusel in his books *Thomas Münzer and his Times (Thomas Münzer und seine Zeit)* and *Thomas Münzer*[3] takes the same view as Engels. At the end of the last-named book Meusel summarises four reasons why Münzer, a positive but unfortunate hero, had outstripped his times. He comments: 'In Münzer's view truth was not in the Bible, nor in the decisions of Church councils, but could be recognized as a process in which every man could participate, if he made the requisite assumptions. Although this idea in Münzer's thought is combined with a lot of mystical embellishments, Engels quite rightly pointed out that Münzer's religious philosophy bordered on atheism.'[4]

In much the same way since Engels but before Meusel the Soviet

[1] Engels, *The Peasant War in Germany* (ET by M. J. Olgin), London 1927, p. 66.
[2] Wilhelm Zimmermann, *Allgemeine Geschichte der grossen Bauernkriege*, 1840-43; *Der grosse deutsche Bauernkrieg* (popular edition), Berlin 1953.
[3] A. Meusel, *Thomas Münzer und seine Zeit*, Berlin 1952; *Thomas Münzer*, Leipzig/Jena, 1956.
[4] Meusel, *Münzer*, p. 52.

historian M. M. Smirin commended Münzer's re-interpretation of Christianity in his comprehensive work *Thomas Münzer's Account of the Popular Reformation and the Great Peasants' Revolt* (*Die Volksreformation des Thomas Münzer und der grosse Bauernkrieg*): 'Fidelity to God meant for Münzer the complete subordination of all particularity beneath the general world principle. By Christian perfection Münzer understood the active and selfless devotion to the universal principle and the renunciation of all selfish ends.' He maintained that Münzer, in contradiction to Luther, regarded faith not as a passive inner condition, not as a gift of grace, but as active participation in mundane affairs. He rejected humility and passivity. He replaced Christian love, the central point of Lutheran theology, by the fear of God (*timor dei*) by which he understood man's responsibility and his duty to go forward selflessly with the sword of Gideon against all oppressors of the people, who were hindering the establishment of justice on earth. Luther had regarded grace as the supernatural source of faith, whereas Münzer considered faith to be the revelation expressed in the 'inner word' and he interpreted this revelation as the reason of the perfect. Münzer considers the criterion of true reason to be standing up for real social justice, the readiness to fight against oppressors and to build a firm foundation for the common good in the world. The peasants and the poor townspeople possessed true reason and were interested in a real abolition of tyranny.[1]

The teaching of Münzer as presented by Engels, Meusel and Smirin clearly differs profoundly from Luther's, even though the account given by the three authors be very one-sided. The arguments between Luther and Münzer were profound and serious. Münzer's religious philosophy is fanatical and mystical and cannot stand up against the witness of the Bible to God's action in Christ. The truth of Luther's or Münzer's teaching stands or falls with the question of the meaning and authority of the Holy Scriptures. According to this criterion Münzer can rightly be placed in the fanatical tradition, and so amongst the 'enthusiasts' who

---

[1] M. M. Smirin, *Die Volksreformation des Thomas Münzer und der grosse Bauernkrieg*, Berlin 1952, p. 653.

believed that the work of the Holy Spirit was not confined to the intermediation of the Word of God. But although Thomas Münzer did not feel tied to biblical revelation, yet he wanted to remain faithful and obedient to the Holy Spirit as he understood it, so that he cannot be included in a consciously atheistic tradition.

French Atheism in the Eighteenth Century

The French materialists and atheists of the eighteenth century play an important part in the conflict with religion. Friedrich Engels quickly recognized their significance for the overthrow of Christianity. In a newspaper article of 26th June, 1874 he recommended 'that efforts should be made to see that the excellent French materialistic literature of the previous century should be widely distributed amongst the workers, the literature in which the French sense of form and content had so far found its highest achievement, and which, allowing for the then state of scientific knowledge, is still valuable in content today, and in form has never been equalled.'[1]

With reference to these words of Engels Lenin wrote in March 1922 in his monograph *On the Significance of Militant Atheism*, in which he advocated a periodical as the organ of militant materialism and atheism: 'Engels advised the leaders of the modern proletariat a long time ago to translate for mass distribution the polemic atheistic literature of the late eighteenth century. To our shame we have not yet done this—one of the many proofs that it is a great deal easier to gain power in a revolutionary period than to learn how rightly to use this power.' Lenin refused to accept as excuse for this negligence the plea that the old atheistic literature was out of date, unscientific and naïve. He did not deny that there were unscientific and naïve features in these writings, but he recommended that they should be published in abridged form and with references to the scientific advances since. Then he goes on: 'It would be one of the greatest and most fatal mistakes that a Marxist can make to think that the vast mass of the people, particularly the peasants and artisans, who are condemned by the whole modern social set-up to intellectual darkness, ignorance and

---

[1] Marx-Engels, *On Religion*, p. 141f.

prejudice, could only escape from this darkness along the straight path of pure Marxist enlightenment. These masses must be supplied with atheistic propaganda material of every conceivable sort; they must be made familiar with facts from the most varied spheres of life; every effort must be made to arouse their interest and awaken them from religious sleep, to shake them up in many different ways by the use of the most varied methods.'[1]

In view of these statements of Engels and Lenin it is no longer necessary to work out in detail the contribution made by the French materialists and atheists of the eighteenth century to the atheistic tradition, or to go into their arguments against religion. It will be sufficient to quote a summary formulated by the Soviet author Zebenko, a specialist on this period: 'The outstanding French thinkers of the eighteenth century completed the development of materialism and atheism in the sixteenth and seventeenth centuries and carried materialistic anti-religious philosophy much further. They provided science with a theoretical weapon and created the ideological prerequisites for the further development of materialism in the nineteenth century.'[2] Bearing in mind this atheistic tradition and with a view to the education of social consciousness, individual works and full editions of the French atheists of the eighteenth century are now being mass produced and distributed among the people.[3]

Russian Revolutionary Democrats of the Nineteenth Century

Modern materialistic atheism identifies the atheistic tradition in Russian history also, and finds indications of atheism in the points of view discovered there. A recent article on the subject claims: 'The Russian revolutionary democrats of the nineteenth century, Herzen, Belinski, Chernyshevski, Dobrolyubov, and also Ogaryov, Pissarev and representatives of Russian scientific progress like Sechenov, Mendeleyev, Timiryasev, Pavlov and Michurin made a particularly important contribution to the development of atheism. They waged a ceaseless war on the

---

[1] Lenin, *Religion* (Little Lenin Library, No. 7), London n.d., p. 37.
[2] M. D. Zebenko, *Der Atheismus der französischen Materialisten*, Berlin 1956, p. 3.
[3] Works by and on Diderot, Voltaire, Helvetius and others.

reactionary theories of religious obscurantism and on ecclesiastical orthodoxy. Under the difficult conditions of czarist tyranny they championed progressive atheistic ideas. There was a close connection between the philosophic outlook of the Russian revolutionaries and democrats and their political struggle against the yoke of the landowners and the despotism of czarism that was strangling the people. Their atheistic views found ready acceptance among the people, for they reflected the moods and hopes of the enslaved peasantry. In the struggle against the official ideology of despotism and against the state religion the atheism of the Russian democrats acquired an active militant character.'[1]

The Russian atheists of the nineteenth century, like the French atheists of the eighteenth, made a contribution to the atheistic tradition and added to it political, social and scientific features.

Atheistic Tendencies in Indian and Chinese Philosophy

In its efforts to establish an atheistic tradition modern materialistic atheism does not confine itself to European history. Applying the criterion 'materialism/idealism' it seeks support for its theses in the cultural development of the non-European peoples also.

For example, Walter Ruben in his *History of Indian Philosophy* (*Geschichte der indischen Philosophie*)[2] attempts to describe Indian philosophy from the standpoint of historical materialism, following the guiding principle laid down by Zhdanov, according to which the scientific history of philosophy is primarily the history of the inception, rise and development of materialism and its laws.[3]

The philosophy of ancient China has been examined and evaluated in the same way. A Chinese philosopher, Yang Hsing-Shun has written about the *Conflict of Materialism and Idealism in Ancient China*.[4] Another, Yang Yun-kuo, has written about the *History of Ancient Chinese Ideology*.[5]

Of course, the extraordinary internal difficulties of applying a modern criterion to a past of thousands of years ago and to

[1] Oleshchuk, *Atheismus*, p. 15. Also Pavyolkin and Baskin. [See pp. 57 and 38.]
[2] Walter Ruben, *Geschichte der indischen Philosophie*, Berlin 1954.
[3] Zhdanov, *Kritische Bemerkungen*, p. 6.
[4] Yang Hsing-Shun, 'Der Kampf des Materialismus mit dem Idealismus im alten China', *Deutsche Zeitschrift für Philosophie*, 1954/5/557.
[5] Yang Yun-kuo, *Geschichte der alten Ideologie Chinas*, Peking 1954.

non-european history become obvious here also, because the figures and movements of those times and peoples are not easily fitted into the general philosophic pattern. A Chinese critic, commenting on the attempt to regard Chinese traditions from Zhdanov's angle said that the ideology of the ancient Chinese philosophers is too often condemned or extolled uncritically. 'Any systematic account of the ideology of ancient China is extremely difficult. Which philosophers of Chinese antiquity are, after all, fundamentally materialists? Which philosophers are fundamentally idealists? Any classification of the old beliefs into "streams" and "groups" has to be very critically checked, taking into account what is held to be the main current of progressive materialism. Every ideology is sometimes and in some respects progressive and materialistic but in others reactionary and idealistic. There are some ideologies that are philosophically materialistic but politically very reactionary and *vice versa*. How are these problems to be accurately solved? How are we today to put into proper perspective many ideologies which in the past have been neglected, underestimated, persecuted and ridiculed?'[1]

There are similar difficulties with regard to Indian philosophy. It is a matter of controversy whether Buddhism and Jainism are to be interpreted as progressive or reactionary.

The same difficulties arise even in regard to the atheistic tradition of western lands, not least among the philosophers who laid the foundation of modern anti-religious criticism and so provided a religio-philosophic basis for Ludwig Feuerbach's modern materialistic atheism.

Culmination of the Atheistic Tradition in Feuerbach

The religious philosophy of Ludwig Feuerbach (1804-1872) marked at the same time the culmination and the end of the atheistic tradition. That is still true today, in spite of the fact that present-day materialistic atheism has made serious but abortive efforts to find atheistic tendencies in eighteenth-century Germany. The only evidence produced is a few quotations from insignificant

---

[1] Chou Fu-Chen, review of Yang Yun-kuo's *Geschichte*, *Deutsche Zeitschrift für Philosophie*, 1955/5/652.

authors, such as, for example, an unknown atheist from the beginning of the eighteenth century, who deposited an atheistic pamphlet in St Catherine's Church in Magdeburg on the 15th January 1714,[1] an eclectic philosopher contemporary with Goethe, August von Einsiedel (1754-1837),[2] and finally a minor philosopher named Karl von Knoblauch (1756-1794).[3]

Recently, in order to bolster up the atheistic tradition even a forgery from the seventeenth and eighteenth century has been published, to which further reference is made later.[4]

Thus for present-day materialistic atheism Feuerbach is still the chief authority for the atheistic tradition and the main source for atheistic polemics, because he has set out and elaborated all the arguments that can be produced as the basis of atheism. The thoroughness and consistency with which Feuerbach expounded and elaborated his atheism have not been equalled by any author since. It is on Feuerbach's ideas that present-day materialistic atheism subsists. Hardly a single new original idea has been added to it. Whatever there is scholarly and recondite in modern theoretical atheism is due to Feuerbach and whatever is specious and inflammatory comes from other sources.

Friedrich Engels recognized the great significance of Feuerbach for Marx and himself, and even forty-seven years after the appearance of Feuerbach's main work *The Nature of Christianity* (*Das Wesen des Christentums*) in 1841, he recalled the lasting impression made by it on Marx and himself in the following words: 'Then came Feuerbach's *Nature of Christianity*. With one stroke it pulverized all opposition by putting materialism unequivocally back on the throne. Nature exists independently of all philosophy. It is the foundation on which we men, ourselves the products of nature, grow up. Besides nature and man nothing exists and the supernatural beings whom our imagination created are only the

[1] Gottfried Stiehler, 'Ein vergessener deutscher Atheist vom Beginn des 18. Jahrhunderts', *Deutsche Zeitschrift für Philosophie*, 1955/5/541.

[2] August von Einsiedel, *Ideen*, Berlin 1957; Wilhelm Dobbek, 'August von Einsiedel', *Deutsche Zeitschrift für Philosophie*, 1955/5/557.

[3] Otto Finger, 'Karl von Knoblauch, ein deutscher Atheist des 18. Jahrhunderts', *Deutsche Zeitschrift für Philosophie*, 1958/6/924.

[4] *De tribus impostoribus Anno MDIIC—Von den drei Betrügern 1598* (Moses, Jesus, Mohammed), Berlin 1960.

fancied reflection of ourselves. The spell was broken, the system was exploded and cast aside, the opposition was dispersed as though it had existed only in our imagination. The emancipatory effect of this book had to be experienced personally in order to be appreciated. Enthusiasm was general, we were all for the time Feuerbachians. How enthusiastically Marx welcomed the new ideas and how greatly he was influenced by them, in spite of all critical reservations can be seen from his *Holy Family (Heilige Familie).*[1]

Marx and Engels were influenced throughout their lives by Feuerbach's atheistic religious philosophy and through them Feuerbach's ideas passed into present-day atheism. In recent years Feuerbach's *Nature of Christianity* has been published in two complete editions, one scholarly and the other popular. It is, therefore, true to say that Feuerbach's anti-religious philosophy dominates present-day materialistic atheism, which adheres to his basic thesis: 'No God created man in his own image, as religion, particularly Christianity, Judaism and Islam assert, but on the contrary man has created God in his image.'[2]

Of course Marx and Engels went beyond Feuerbach in some particulars. Marx wanted not only a new interpretation of the world, but above all to change it, as his well-known eleventh thesis on Feuerbach underlines. Nor did Marx regard men just theoretically as natural beings, as did Feuerbach, but understood them as concrete social entities. Basically, however, Marx considered the truth of religion to have been refuted by Feuerbach,[3] and so Feuerbach is honoured today as the greatest philosopher before Marx.

Feuerbach's atheism has thus not only been taken over but carried further, which present-day atheism believed necessary, because Feuerbach in the end inclined towards an idealistic position, groping towards a new religion—the religion of love. The relationship of materialistic atheism to Feuerbach's philosophy is thus not one clear unbroken line, but in fact fragmentary. That is clearly perceptible even in the work of a single author,

---

[1] Engels, *Ludwig Feuerbach*, p. 28.
[2] M. P. Baskin *Materialismus und Religion*, Berlin 1957, p. 76.
[3] Marx-Engels, *On Religion*, p. 70.

Herbert Gute. Writing in 1956, he expressed the criticism that Feuerbach had derived religion from men's wishful thinking. This Gute rejected, and yet in a book written in 1958 he recognized Feuerbach's religious philosophy as the precursor of that of Engels.[1]

To sum up it can be said that Feuerbach's atheism marks the culmination and the end of the atheistic tradition—not the end in the sense of atheism being abandoned, but being raised to a new and higher level, that of being 'scientifically and materialistically based'.

Standpoints from which the Atheistic Tradition is open to Criticism

The outline that has been sketched of the atheistic tradition, which might be entitled 'From Prometheus to Feuerbach' covers a period from the mythical beginning of systematic thought up to the threshold of modern times. This atheistic tradition will be further illustrated by a few brief observations and its philosophic value assessed in a few critical notes.

1. The Atheistic Tradition has been broadened in some Fields

The account already given of the atheistic tradition has only indicated a few general features in order to give an overall picture of the main historical periods and the principal figures. Even in this limited survey the wealth of material brought forward in support of an atheistic tradition and the depth of the problems involved are impressive enough, but modern atheists discover in history tendencies, which admittedly do not imply thorough-going atheism, but yet point the way towards it. For example, the overall picture of the atheistic tradition becomes still more complicated by the inclusion of the various sects (Montanists and others), and one or two pre-Reformation movements, which have grown up on Christian soil and have torn the Christian Church asunder, are particularly popular with materialistic atheism, because they are regarded as a counterpoise to the great churches. Engels put forward

[1] Gute-Ritter, *Glauben oder Wissen*, Berlin 1956, p. 23; H. Gute, *Glauben oder Wissen*, Berlin 1958, p. 27.

this idea and Kautsky in his book *Forerunners of Modern Socialism* (*Vorläufer des neueren Sozialismus*), 1894, worked it out more thoroughly. More recently the German mystics (Meister Eckhart, Seuse, and others) have been similarly interpreted, together with Joachim von Fiore (1132-1202) the founder of a monastic order, and the Hussites, the Taborites[1] and the Adamites. These last were two sects in the fourteenth and fifteenth centuries. Besides these a new book has appeared on the Circumcellions by Theodora Büttner[2] pointing in the same direction.

In the effort to work out an atheistic tradition materialistic atheism does not confine itself to genuinely atheistic beliefs but makes use of any aberrations in faith or order, that tend to disturb, or in some cases destroy, the faith based on the Bible. These tendencies and movements are no longer dismissed as 'secret church' but are interpreted and welcomed as an embryonic 'counter-church'.

2. *The Atheistic Tradition has been extended to all areas of Culture*

The criterion materialism/idealism is applied not only to history and philosophy but to all other departments of culture. It is surprising to find reference made to the conflict of materialism and idealism in Mathematics, particularly in the calculation of probabilities, or to read of the atheistic significance of Physics and of progressive currents in Astronomy. In Cosmogony theories about the permanence or impermanence of the universe are naturally discussed with particular vigour. In their supposedly atheistic implications the biological sciences, the theories of Darwin and Haeckel[3]

[1] Especially Smirin, *Die Volksreformation des Thomas Münzer.*
[2] Buttner-Werner, *Circumcellionen und Adamiten*, Berlin 1959.
[3] According to a Soviet press handout, 10/1/1958, Charles Darwin's Memoirs were published for the first time in Moscow. Their translator is of opinion that Darwin was by temperament an atheist. Haeckel's position is disputed. The editor of the extracts from Haeckel's writings, *The Riddle of the World* (*Die Welträtsel*—Gibt es ein Weiterleben nach dem Tode?), Berlin 1958, who incidentally took considerable liberties with Haeckel's text, avoids the question, but rounds off Haeckel's statements on the basis of Marxist-Leninist theory. Olof Klohr writes: 'Ernst Haeckel—an atheistic scientist' (*Neues Deutschland*, 12/4/58) while Professor G. Schneider, Director of the Ernst Haeckel House at Jena, thinks Haeckel himself was not an atheist, but by the founding of the '*Monistenbund*' in 1906 had encouraged the materialistic-atheistic movement. A conference on Haeckel decided that he was an atheist. The book *Wunderglaube—Gott—Unsterblichkeit* published in Berlin in 1959 containing extracts from Haeckel is intended as atheistic propaganda.

and Pavlov's Physiology (1849-1936)[1] are similarly expounded and elaborated.

Working out an atheistic tradition within the natural sciences is, of course, very much more difficult than in the humanities, because the natural sciences are primarily concerned with factual evidence and demonstrable realities, so that in their case tendentious forces and stresses are less obvious or easier to see through than in the humanities. Thus it is easier to apply the atheistic criterion in the case of those sciences which are more philosophically and ethically conditioned than in the case of the natural sciences: for instance in Pedagogy, Literature and Art. Here, too, an attempt is made from the atheistic standpoint to discover an atheistic tradition, its origin, development and possibilities. In these social sciences and their history the criterion of 'progress' is given an atheistic content as in the history of philosophy.

In the history of Pedagogy, for example, efforts are made to find these 'progressive' elements in Comenius (1592-1670), Pestalozzi (1746-1827), Froebel (1782-1852), Diesterweg (1790-1866), Wander (1803-1879) and others,[2] but in most cases with very little success. In this connection Christian factors in theoretical Pedagogy and practical education and everything connected with them are particularly sharply criticized and the effects of empirical and realistic factors exaggerated as evidence of definitely materialistic views, in order to make the history and science of education support only the 'progressive' atheistic beliefs.

3. The Atheistic Tradition is Ambiguous

At first sight the materialistic-atheistic tradition presents a compact and uniform picture. Closer inspection, however, reveals that it has no uniform structure, either as regards the tendencies leading to atheism or the actual positive exemplification of the basic idea. The systematic picture of world history, reminiscent of Hegel, is certainly impressive, but it is impossible to develop it

---

[1] See article by Shorochova in *Natur, Mensch und Religion*, Berlin 1958.

[2] *Geschichte der Erziehung*, Berlin 1957; Robert Alt, *Der fortschrittliche Charakter der Pädagogik Komenskys*, Berlin 1953: Robert Alt, *Johannes Heinrich Pestalozzi*, Berlin/Leipzig, 1951; *Gedenkschrift zum 100 Todestag von Friedrich Fröbel*, Berlin 1952; Hans Siebert, *Adolph Diesterweg*, Berlin 1953; *K. F. W. Wander*, Berlin 1954.

completely, since it often does violence to real historical figures and periods.

The tradition worked out by materialistic atheism is ambiguous, because it applies to the figures and periods of times past and to remote peoples, the modern European criterion materialism/idealism, which is and must remain foreign to them. It finds its origin and ancestors not in science but in myth (Prometheus, Heraclitus, Euhemeros and Lucretius).

Its judgment of the philosophers of Greece, India and China can only be a partial one, because their philosophical and political attitude measured by the criterion of 'progress' in the philosophical sense of the twentieth century, is mostly inconsistent. Even in relation to the Renaissance and to Feuerbach's philosophy of religion this criterion is only applicable to some few aspects and cannot lead to an unambiguous verdict. The reason for the ambiguity of the atheistic tradition lies in the fact that the criterion employed cannot be objectively established but is predominantly conditioned by its values.

4. *The Atheistic Tradition is Tendentious*

Materialistic atheism does not study history in order to form a picture of the past, but to find weapons to use against religion. Consequently the tradition which is built up is not an end in itself but the means to an end in the fight against religion, hence its significance nowadays.

In an essay on 'Lenin's struggle for the progressive philosophical inheritance of mankind' there are references on the one hand to the continuity and progressive importance of materialism and science, and on the other hand to the reactionary tradition of idealism, religion and mysticism. This shows clearly the tendentious purpose of the exposition of the atheistic tradition. Modern materialism claims to be continuing the struggle against religion and idealism begun by Democritus two thousand years ago. 'In this struggle dialectical materialism, which represents the point of view of the progressive revolutionary class in the modern world, is based on the latest achievements of science, the critical refutation of idealism and on the clear and profound ideas which the materialists

of antiquity, the French atheists of the eighteenth century, Feuerbach, Chernyshevski and other representatives of militant materialism have put forward in its defence.'[1]

This view of the materialistic-atheistic tradition shows that it has
not been worked out as a disinterested plan, but as an important
part of the battle against religion. History is thus enlisted in the
service and under the banner of atheism. The atheistic tradition is
used by modern atheists as the foundation and endorsement of
the basic principles of atheism.

5. *The Atheistic Tradition so interprets History as to reduce Its Meaning*

In its quest for an atheistic tradition in history materialistic
atheism turns its attention to the backward peoples and particularly
the asiatics, but its principle of selection narrows the wide scope
and variety of history by frequently over-estimating unimportant
things and under-estimating some important ones. The standard
of values which its principle of selection assumes, namely that
idealism is error and evil, while materialism is right and good,
over-simplifies the problem and dismisses the real question by
affixing a label. History and life are richer than any pattern or
principle. Sweeping generalizations may be useful in assisting
selection and evaluation of evidence but they restrict and distort
real life and history. Just as every individual human being has
also personal direct access to God and cannot be understood and
judged only by his natural situation, so every historical figure and
every historical period has its own peculiarity, that extends beyond
any pattern or principle.

The limitation and reinterpretation of history by materialistic
atheism is clearly seen in the fact that it interprets in a 'progressive'
sense periods and figures in world history, which are universally
admired and either cites them as pioneers of materialism and atheism or deprives them of their real significance and motives. It
does not hesitate to reinterpret even the figures of Christianity in
the sense of 'progress'.

[1] M. T. Yovchuk, and M. I. Sidorov, 'Lenins Kampf für das fortschrittliche
philosophische Erbe der Menschheit', *Deutsche Zeitschrift für Philosophie*,
1955/1/59.

Thus the story of the passion of Jesus is not accepted as what the unanimous testimony of the four evangelists would have us believe, but is interpreted only as an example of standing up for one's convictions and as self-sacrifice for the good of the people. Similarly the breakdown of the discussion between Luther and Zwingli in 1529 about the Lord's Supper is not considered to be due to theological reasons but to social causes: the progressive-bourgeois tendencies of the Swiss Reformation were irreconcilable with the feudal-absolutist content of Lutheran theology; the cause lay in the backwardness of the central and north German middle class.[1] Similarly the directly Christian elements in the creative achievements of Dürer, Bach and Handel are disregarded, and they are applauded simply as secular artists, who for economic reasons had to adapt their works to the Church and to the spirit of the times. Again the whole Lutheran Reformation is wrongly interpreted by claiming that Luther's religion had instilled into the people as the most important article of faith: 'Submit yourselves to authority.'[2]

6. The Question of Criterion

These last examples particularly, with their peculiar reasoning, are closely connected with the principle of selection and standard of values. Whatever epochs, figures and ideas the atheistic tradition may include, the decision as to its truth and present-day validity does not lie within it but outside it. The criterion laid down by Engels and taken over by Zhdanov cannot be maintained on the grounds of history and events alone, because it is based, not on objective viewpoints, but on subjective values.

Marx very early began to seek the 'idea' in the 'real'.[3] Later he regarded the truth of religion as having been refuted,[4] and eventually said that the most important achievement of German philosophy was its criticism of religion—here he obviously meant

---

[1] Hanna Koditz, 'Die gesellschaftlichen Ursachen des Marburger Religionsgesprächs vom 1 bis 4 Oktober 1529', *Deutsche Zeitschrift für Philosophie*, 1954/1/37.

[2] Alexander Abusch, *Der Irrweg einer Nation, Ein Beitrag zum Verständnis deutscher Geschichte*, Berlin 1951, p. 24f.

[3] Karl Marx, letter to his father, 10/11/1837.

[4] Marx-Engels, *On Religion*, p. 41.

refutation.[1] In the same sense Engels said that the French spirit had reached its greatest achievement from the point of view of content and form, in the atheistic literature of the eighteenth century; with regard to content it still (1174) stood extremely high, and in form it had never since been equalled.[2]

It must be said therefore that the criterion used by materialistic atheism to establish the tradition it desires is not provided by history itself, but arises from another source, namely from a philosophic-atheistic prejudice. This was subsequently applied to history in order to extract from it the ideas which support atheistic views. The question as to the validity and truth of the atheistic tradition is thus driven into a deeper dimension that will be discussed later.

7. History and Tradition as the Area of conflict between Evangelical Faith and Materialistic Atheism

Materialistic atheism, which likes to consider itself a scientific philosophy, seeks the roots of its own tradition, not in science, but in the mythical ideas of the early philosophers. At the same time it objects to a literal interpretation of the meagre sources and quotations and insists on their being understood and interpreted in a general sense, in order thus to use them as evidence for the atheistic tradition and to support present-day atheism. On the other hand, it passionately resists any interpretation of religion, Christianity and the Bible according to their spirit, in order by literal interpretation to reduce them to absurdity. It fails to look at religion and faith as a coherent whole, and thus misses the essential reality.

The inescapable conclusion from this is that history and tradition do not furnish accurate and objective knowledge, but provide the arena for the conflict between faith and atheism. The question of the truth and accuracy of the tradition, whether Christian or atheistic, is not an isolated entity, nor is it objectively determinable, but demands its own act of faith and commitment, both of which are involved in every case. The existence of the

---

[1] *Marx-Engels Gesamtausgabe*, I 6, p. 639.
[2] Marx-Engels, *On Religion*, p. 142.

Christian faith cannot be substantiated either by philosophy or history alone, and so cannot be refuted by them. It is sustained from other sources and cannot therefore be overturned by an atheistic tradition, even if in the future that tradition should have brought into it still more periods and figures than hitherto. The conflicting traditions stand or fall with the reality to which they testify, and this is disclosed not in history alone, but in the profounder dimension of faith.

2 · Materialistic Atheism on Religion

THERE ARE TWO REASONS WHY MATERIALISTIC ATHEISM concerns itself with religion, one theoretical and one practical. In the first place its own basic beliefs about the material nature of the world and how it is to be explained lead it to examine all available phenomena and to try to find a scientific explanation for everything. But it is just in its investigation of history and its examination of the present situation that it comes up against the phenomena of religion and Christianity, faith and the Church, and because of its own presuppositions it has to define its attitude to them, if it does not wish to leave something unexplained.

So atheism does not simply reject religion; it tries to find the causes for its existence, the laws of its development and its essential nature, not in order to understand it, but in order to attack it, refute it and finally to destroy it. For it senses a dilemma in which we as human beings are involved and which we cannot avoid: either there is truth in religion, which although often distorted and confused by human frailties, nevertheless points definitely enough to the existence of God, or 'there is no God' and religion should be swept away along with 'superstition', 'mysticism' and 'obscurantism'. But as long as faith and religion, Church and the Bible exist, materialistic atheism feels insecure and threatened in its basic presuppositions. In this sense religion is a serious and final opponent of atheism.

Development of the Atheistic Conception of Religion from Euhemeros to Lenin

Materialistic atheism has developed various ideas about religion, but underlying all of them is the insistence that religion is a human invention, the product of imagination and wishful thinking, and has no objective reality.

This is not a modern idea; its roots can be traced back into ancient mythology of Egypt and Greece. It found its first recognizable expression in Euhemeros of Messina (*c.* 300 BC) a disciple of Aristippus of Cyrene, who in turn was a pupil and friend of Socrates. In his well-known work *Sacred History* (*Hiera Anagraphe*), which he wrote in the form of a travelogue, he tells of the finding of a column on which was an inscription revealing that the gods Uranus, Chronos and Zeus had been heroic personalities of earlier days. On account of their distinction they had come to be worshipped as gods. This interpretation by Euhemeros of the Greek hierarchy of gods discredited them and even threatened their existence. This rational pragmatic explanation of the gods was received with great sympathy by the contemporary Greeks, because several Greek kings had demanded divine honours for themselves and so had followed the same path that Zeus and the other gods were supposed to have taken in earlier times.

In the nineteenth century Ludwig Feuerbach adopted as the basis of his philosophy of religion Euhemeros' contention that religion and the world of gods had been a human invention. To him the content and substance of religion were entirely human. The key to the mystery of the divine being was the human being, the secret of theology was anthropology. In religion man projected his own nature or nature itself into something superhuman and supernatural. Feuerbach's central idea, expressed in his most important works *The Nature of Christianity* (*Das Wesen des Christentums*, 1841) and *The Nature of Religion* (*Das Wesen der Religion*, 1845), reverses the biblical statement 'God created man in his own image' (Gen. 1.27) into 'Man created God in his own image.'[1]

Karl Marx adopted Feuerbach's anthropocentric principle,

[1] Hence the title of the Werner Schuffenhauer Selection from Feuerbach.

borrowed from Euhemeros, and formulated it thus: 'The basis of anti-religious criticism is that man makes religion, religion does not make man.'[1] Engels expressed the same idea in this way: 'Now all religion is nothing else but the imaginative reflection in the minds of men of those external forces which control their daily lives, a reflection in which natural forces take on the form of the supernatural.'[2]

Similarly, Lenin regarded religion as a human invention when he wrote: 'The powerlessness of the exploited classes in the struggle against the exploiters inevitably aroused belief in a better life beyond, just as the powerlessness of savages in the struggle against nature awakens belief in gods, devils, miracles, etc.'[3] The same idea of religion lies at the root of another statement of Lenin: 'God is above all a complex of ideas produced by man's apathetic sense of oppression both by external nature and by the class system, and these ideas tend to perpetuate this sense of oppression and weaken the class struggle.'[4]

These are in outline the critical ideas of materialistic atheism from Feuerbach to Lenin. They are set forth in modern atheism with minor variations and comment as proven, without fresh arguments. According to the circumstances they may be explicit or implicit, but the basic line is unaltered. Hardly any new elements have been introduced by modern atheistic writers; at the most they have attempted to interpret modern events in the light of Feuerbach's views. In fact everything essential was said by Feuerbach, and his views represent the fundamental question and the atheistic answer. However much the view of religion taken by Feuerbach and Marx, Engels and Lenin, may vary in details, however the motives and methods of their conflict with religion and Christianity may differ, they are all agreed on one point: materialistic atheism regards religion fundamentally as a human invention, as a creation of the brain, as a form of social consciousness, as a complex, as a utopian illusion, and so as the fanciful product of a false view of reality. But as religion has existed for a long time and is widespread over the whole earth,

---

[1] Marx-Engels, *On Religion*, p. 41. [2] *Op. cit.*, p. 146.
[3] Lenin, *Religion*, p. 11. [4] *Op. cit.*, p. 53.

materialistic atheism feels bound to explain its origin and development and to attempt its defeat. Thus in order to maintain the credibility of its own philosophic basis it is forced to discuss the origin and nature of religion.

Materialistic Atheism on the Origin of Religion

Materialistic atheism has a definite interest in elucidating the origin of religion. The obvious intention is by discrediting its origin to discredit religion itself. For this reason it is not only concerned with the analysis of religion as it exists at the present time, but investigates its roots also. That is why in its conflict with religion the question of its origin occupies so much space.

In 1956 N. N. Rosental wrote in considerable detail on the subject 'How religious concepts arose'.[1] He distinguished a 'pre-religious phase in the history of man' from a later period which he calls the period of 'conditions favourable to the rise of religion'. These conditions had been created primarily by the development of abstract thinking, reflecting reality in general concepts. The complicated nature of this thought process encouraged a distorted image of reality and produced, as Lenin said, the epistemological roots of a religio-idealistic view of the world.

According to Rosental, primitive man was thoroughly oppressed by the hard struggle against nature. He was very ignorant and pictured to himself the mysterious and terrible forces of nature as powerful spirits and supernatural powers. One of the earliest forms of such a distorted image of reality was the endowment of natural objects and natural phenomena with human characteristics. This was not yet religion. The prior constituents of every religion were first animism and later totemism, the fantastic belief in mysterious and unseen beings. At a later stage these beings and spirits were called gods. In this way men created in their own imagination various kinds of supernatural beings.

Rosental goes on: Religion not only invented some sort of supernatural world, but also provided rituals by which to influence the spirits and the gods (rise of Magic). The religion that arose in

[1] *Soviet Union Press (SUP)*, issued by the government News Bureau of the East German Republic, 1956/18/431.

this way influenced all other forms of social consciousness, particularly art and morals. By placing its stamp on the whole of life, religion misrepresented man's environment, undermined his belief in his own strength, and fixed permanently in his mind his sense of helplessness in the face of nature. Since then all forms of religious belief have exercised a reactionary influence, because they have hindered man's struggle with nature, the development of human knowledge and social progress.

From the hierarchy of more powerful and less powerful gods, in Rosental's view, the concept of a single supreme god arose. The further development of the religious cult and the worship of the gods had been due to churches and priestly castes. In the classless society it was the natural forces, in the class society the social forces, that were reflected in religion. Religion became a tool in the hands of the ruling classes and a means of gagging the minds of the masses. The doctrine of eternal life as a compensation for misery endured on earth restrained the exploited masses from fighting for their real interests. They were taught to endure their servitude with humility and resignation. Only the victory of socialism would abolish the exploitation of man by man, eradicate the social roots of religion and create the conditions for its complete extinction.

Rosental's view of the origin of religion is not without a certain imaginative force. It starts from the fundamental idea developed by the earlier materialistic atheists, but then it leaves open the vital question whether the actual historical religions did in fact originate in this way. Rosental sees an important presupposition for the existence of religion in the development of abstract thinking, obviously because in this way religion can be explained as the product of the brain, a process within the human mind. Here he agrees with other writers who consider religion to be a comparatively late product of human society,[1] repudiate any innate religious feeling,[2] and deny the existence of any 'natural religion'.[3]

[1] H. Scheler, *Die Stellung des Marxismus-Leninismus zur Religion*, Berlin 1957, p. 8.

[2] M. S. Butinova and U. Seemann.

[3] G. A. Kursanov, p. 187. 'Das reaktionäre Wesen der "natürlichen" Religion', *SUP*, 1958/46/983 (20/4/58).

Here, however, a difference of opinion arises within the ranks of materialistic atheism, on this very question whether there was any kind of religion in the earliest stages of human development, in primitive society. While Heinrich Eildermann (1921) thought that the oldest religious notions arose with the beginning of social differences,[1] P. P. Cherkashkin (1958) vigorously opposes the assertion that the social roots of religion only developed with the division of society into antagonistic classes and asserts that previously, namely in primitive society, religion had no social basis.[2] In this difference, not very important in itself, it is evident that some of the materialistic theorists regard religion as having its origin primarily in social conditions, while others find its roots mainly in rational grounds. A third view, represented by M. S. Butinova derives religion from the axiom: As the way of living so the way of thinking. The living conditions of primitive men gave rise to their religious beliefs: the feeling of powerlessness against the forces of nature which governed their existence aroused in men of primitive times erroneous notions about the world; those forces assumed in their minds the fanciful form of supernatural beings.[3] Butinova's theory agrees with Rosental, but differs in regarding these beliefs as religious.

Materialistic Atheism on the Roots of Religion

In the relevant literature of materialistic atheism frequent references are made to the 'roots', 'sources' and 'causes' of religion. It is possible to distinguish four different roots of religion in the atheistic views.

1. The Economic Roots of Religion

Historic materialism seeks the ultimate grounds of all the phenomena of social life, and thus also of the origin and spread of religious ideas, theories and currents, not in the minds of men, but in economic conditions and in the class struggle that these cause and determine. According to Engels economic conditions are 'in

[1] H. Eildermann, *Die Urgesellschaft*, Berlin 1950, p. 419.

[2] Cherkashkin, *Über die sozialen Wurzeln der Religion*.

[3] Butinova. 'Leben und Glaubensvorstellungen von Volkerstämmen der Vorzeit', *SUP*, 1956/62/1462.

the final analysis the vital causative factor, the scarlet thread running through everything and the sole guide to understanding'.[1] On the principle that 'what is determines beliefs' the conclusion is drawn that in the end the material economic living conditions determine religion also. Engels, Kautsky, Mehring and others emphasise 'the economic basis of the history of religion'.[2] Similarly Ulrich Seemann stresses the dependence of religion on the economic conditions in a society,[3] and Scheler is of the opinion that the transition from polytheism to henotheism was the religious reflection of the cultural development of the peoples of antiquity and their political structures, and that the essential content of modern Christianity is determined by a capitalist society.[4]

2. The Rational Roots of Religion

Tracing the rational roots of religion also plays an important part in materialistic atheism, but the question remains open whether the more important roots of religion are to be found in man's mind or in the economic conditions under which he lives. The idea of understanding and explaining religion rationally is a legacy from the rationalism preserved by Kant, Hegel and Feuerbach. Even the view of primitive religion described by Marx and Engels regards religion primarily as a rational category, often even as a rival contributor to knowledge and epistemology. In reference to both subjects, religion and knowledge, the term 'reflected image' is frequently used, so that they are often given the same function. The difference then consists not in the reflected object—that could only be one and the same, namely reality—but only in the quality of the reflected image: knowledge (science) gave a true image of reality, whereas religion gave a false, unreal and fanciful image of it. Thus materialistic atheists in demonstrating the rational roots of religion stress the distortion of reality that it produces.

Religion is also regarded as man's attempt to explain and interpret the world around him. Hence they assume the ability for

[1] Marx-Engels, *Selected Correspondence* (Foreign Languages Publishing House, Moscow), No. 234, p. 549.
[2] Mehring, *Über den historischen Materialismus*, Berlin 19, p. 107.
[3] Seemann, 'Frühe Wurzeln der Religion', *Neues Deutschland*, 6/12/58.
[4] Scheler, *Die Stellung*, p. 12.

abstract thought. They regard the mind as the seat of religion, hence the frequent connection of religion with concepts of the mind, imagination and prejudice. Hence too the frequent references to rational processes in the attempt to defeat religion: scientific enlightenment, change of mind, etc. The complicated nature of the process of knowing made possible both true and false judgments, images and opinions. Real knowledge, confirmed by experience and scientifically assured, is taken by materialistic atheism as the criterion distinguishing truth and falsehood.

3. The Dynamic Roots of Religion

Alongside the economic and rational roots of religion materialistic atheism mentions the helplessness of primitive man against nature and of modern man against the power of capitalism, what may be briefly termed the 'dynamic' roots of religion. Under the heading are included objective and subjective powerlessness and helplessness, individual and collective natural and social hardships, fear, want and misery.

As in the case of the exposition of the rational and economic roots of religion there is also a certain tension between the account given of the dynamic roots on the one hand and the economic and rational roots on the other. Oleshchuk expressed this tension clearly when he said that it was not true that the cause of the rise of the fanciful and distorted beliefs of religion was to be found in men's ignorance, for a considerable number of educated people are religious. It is rather to be found in living conditions. The pressure of the forces of nature and later the pressures of social and class structures were the deepest causes that arouse and nourish religious ideas in the mind.[1]

Thus according to Oleshchuk fear and helplessness should be the real roots of religion. Here Oleshchuk agrees with Lenin's emphasis on the motive: helplessness in the face of nature and society. Lenin took over and emphasised the Latin proverb 'Fear created the gods.'[2] But on the other hand Lenin also stressed very strongly the rational and social roots of religion:

[1] Oleshchuk, 'Wissenschaft und Religion', *SUP*, 1954/100, p. 1154.
[2] Lenin, *Religion*, p. 19.

'The deepest sources of religious prejudice are poverty and ignorance.'[1]

4. The Social Roots of Religion

Although materialistic atheism mentions yet a fourth variety of roots of religion, which may be called the social roots, these too are related to those previously mentioned. The social roots involve not only religion as a form of social as distinct from individual consciousness, but also the determining influence of social conditions on the rise and development of religion. Engels worked out these social conditions particularly for the Christian religion and drew attention to the social misery of the masses in the Roman state. Lenin considered the social roots of religion to be the most important in the capitalist period. Thus, whereas in the early stages of human history and the rise of religion the rational roots are stressed, the social roots are given greater significance for the 'continuation of religion even in the "enlightened" period of modern capitalistic society.'[2]

5. The Multiplicity of Roots of Religion

In the theoretical representation of the idea of religion by materialistic atheism the various roots of religion can be distinguished, but in the practical treatment of religion and in the polemic against it these roots are regarded as related. Hence we often meet several of these roots combined together, for example in Cherkashchin, who considers that the intellectual yoke, i.e. religion, was superimposed on the economic and political yoke.

To consider these various roots of religion in relation to each other, and to attempt to assess their actual effective influence, it would be necessary to examine the individual roots historically and philosophically and in the actual history of the individual religions. This would require a special religio-philosophical and religio-historical investigation of considerable scope, beyond the limits of the present enquiry.

[1] *Op. cit.*, p. 55.   [2] Scheler, *Die Stellung*, p. 16.

Materialistic Atheism on the Content and Function of Religion

Materialistic atheism considers the rise and nature of religion in a narrow context, namely in relation to its theory of the reciprocal action of all phenomena of nature and society. It sees the rise of religion in the same way as it sees its nature, and *vice versa*, and so believes it has understood both fundamentally. Marx and Engels, following Feuerbach, have said the final word on this, which modern atheistic authors only repeat with various comments.

In an early work (1843-4) Karl Marx expressed his famous definition thus: 'Religious misery is at once the expression of material misery and also a protest against it. Religion is the sigh of the oppressed creature, "the heart of a heartless world". It is the soul of soulless conditions. It is the opium of the people. The abolition of religion as the illusory happiness of the people is the demand for its real happiness. The demand to give up illusions about its condition is the demand to abolish conditions that need illusions. The criticism of religion is in effect the criticism of the vale of misery with its nimbus of religion.'[1]

Lenin took over this idea from Marx and underlined it when he wrote in 1909, 'Religion is the opium of the people—this saying of Marx is the cornerstone of the whole Marxist philosophy in relation to religion.'[2]

It is therefore worth while to consider this saying of Karl Marx carefully. Then it loses the terror that it has often aroused and raises the question of the truth and meaning not only of religion but of man's existence in general. The question at issue is: If religion is only the expression of actual misery and a protest against it, how can this misery really be overcome, and is real happiness possible of attainment at all?

Engels tried to explain the idea of religion from a different point of view from that of Marx. He does not start, as Marx does, from actual misery, from which Marx develops the idea of religion, but he regards religion primarily as a fanciful reflection of external forces which assume the form of supernatural powers. At the

---

[1] Marx-Engels, *On Religion*, p. 42.   [2] Lenin, *Religion*, p. 16.

beginning of history it was first of all forces of nature that had been personified, but soon alongside the forces of nature social forces exerted their influence. The fanciful figures which at first had only reflected the forces of nature acquired social attributes and became reflections of historical forces. At a later stage of development all the natural and social attributes of the many gods were transferred to one all-powerful god, who was himself in turn only the reflection of man in the abstract. Thus monotheism had arisen, which was historically the end-product of later Greek popular philosophy and found its embodiment in the Jews' exclusive, national God, Yahweh.

What Engels is saying here about the origin and nature of religion is in essence putting into concrete form the idea of the rational roots of religion. But he adds a psychological factor by the use of the term 'reflection'. Accordingly Engels regards the nature of religion primarily as a process of the mind, which takes the surrounding reality and transforms it into fanciful non-existent powers and forces, spirits and supernatural beings.

Lenin, in his definition of the content of religion, combined several roots together. Historically and from experience of life the idea of God has as ingredients: belief in spirits, prejudices, the sanctification of ignorance and submission on the one hand and slavery and monarchy on the other.[1]

What Marx and Engels specified as the content and function of religion is accepted and systematized by modern atheistic literature but not justified. Thus Pavyolkin says: 'Religion is the belief in supernatural powers and the worship of them. The essence of religion consists in the fact that men invent and create in their imagination immaterial beings (good and evil spirits, angels, devils, satyrs, penates, the immortal soul, etc.) and bow down to them and worship them and observe special rites in their honour.'[2] Similarly he says in another place: 'Religion consists in the belief in supernatural beings and performing religious rites in their honour. The sum total of the religious rites forms the religious cult.'[3] Of course, he admits, like any other mental concept, religion

[1] *Op. cit.*, p. 53.
[2] P. Pavyolkin, *Der religiöse Aberglaube und seine Schädlichkeit*, Berlin 1954, p. 5.
[3] *Op. cit.*

has a basis in reality, but this is so fantastically distorted that it conveys a completely false image of reality. 'Thus religion is a reflection of reality, but an illusory and fanciful reflection. Religion gives a phantastic picture of reality and at the same time gives a double image of the world. Alongside the real objective world it creates an illusory fictitious world of gods and other similar spirits, alongside the terrestrial realm a heavenly kingdom, paradise, hell, etc.'[1]

It is on this view that the estimation of religion by materialistic atheism rests. Although it may sometimes grant religion some justification in its early stages, yet its verdict on religion in our day is destructive. Lenin wrote as long ago as 1909: 'Marxism always regards all present-day religions and churches and all sorts of religious organizations as organs of bourgeois reaction, aimed at the preservation of exploitation, and the confusion of the working class.'[2] In similar vein Hermann Scheler writing on religion devoted a special section to the class function of religion under capitalism. He considers that religion has been the most important ideological means of domination since the beginning of the class struggle, providing moral sanction for misery, exploitation and oppression in the world. 'Religion is able to exercise its class function in the perpetuation of the oppressed classes, by keeping men in ignorance, superstition and fear, by destroying the confidence of the masses in their own strength and by preaching helplessness in the face of the divine will.'[3] Even the Christian religion deserves this stern condemnation, according to Scheler.

What is the Verdict on the Theory and Criticism of Religion by Materialistic Atheism?

The wealth of material produced by materialistic atheism for the understanding of religion makes it difficult to reach an accurate assessment and to arrive at a just verdict, and it is essential to do

---

[1] *Op. cit.*, p. 10f; 'Lehrbuch der deutschen Geschichte' (Beiträge, vol. 1: *Deutschland in der Epoche der Urgesellschaft*, Berlin 1960, p. 30) stresses ignorance as the root of religion. It maintains that religion arose during the transition to the neo-paleolithic period 'due to mistaken ideas originating in the forests about the nature of man and his natural environment' (Engels).

[2] Lenin, *Religion*, p. 16.   [3] Scheler, *Die Stellung*, p. 17.

both. From all the space devoted to religion by materialistic atheism it is clear that it regards religion as an opponent worthy of serious attention involving the fundamental question of truth and reality. But when a Christian considers the subject of 'Atheism and Religion', it is clear, or should be so, that the Gospel is not religion in the sense that theism uses the word, but it is the word of judgment and reconciliation spoken by God to the world. The Christian knows that Jesus Christ means the abolition, the end of religion and at the same time something different and new in the world. Therefore to him religion is not the main question, but is a peripheral matter, an epiphenomenal problem. The Christian faith does not stand or fall with religion, but with the Lord Jesus Christ. Therefore, the Christian can express an opinion with greater freedom on what materialistic atheism has said about religion.

1. Materialistic Atheism forms an Abstract Idea of Religion, which it Derives from the Prior Concept of Idealism

Gagarin began his monograph on Christianity with the sentence: 'Christianity is, like Buddhism, Islam and Judaism, one of the so-called world religions.'[1] Pavyolkin produced in support of his statements about religion the most diverse evidence from all possible periods and kinds of religion. He lumped together quite happily polytheism, the 'Christ legend', Allah, Buddha and Poseidon, Zeus, Neptune and Nicholas. Thus materialistic atheism concocts a general collective idea of religion in the abstract, which does not distinguish between one concrete religion and another. Such a general idea of religion is however hardly possible. There is no such thing as 'universal' religion, but only various world religions. The earlier and modern religions differ so widely in level, in structure and in content, that a general abstraction is only possible if the essential features of the individual religions are ignored.

The existing religions not only defy any abstract generalizations but also cannot be derived from some major category such as idealism. In the view of materialistic atheism idealism, religion

---

[1] A. P. Gagarin, *Die Entstehung und der Klassencharakter des Christentums*, Berlin 1955, p. 3.

and Christianity may be regarded as on the same level, but the obvious thing about Christianity, not only in its modern form, but from the beginning, is that it cannot be derived from the concept of religion or idealism, but insists on being taken for something different, something new, namely historically as consequential on the death and resurrection of our Lord Jesus Christ, and also prophetically on the hope of his return. But this means in effect that the lumping together of idealism, religion, and Christianity is untenable, and that instead a more exact study of the Gospel is necessary, both in its personal and also its external aspects.

Both points of view, the formation of a comprehensive category of religion and its derivation from a prior concept, are clearly evident, when materialistic atheism compares the value of its own attitude with the supposed attitude of religion. Atheism attributes to itself all the virtues, such as the true reflection of reality, reliable judgment, science, dynamic and progress. At the same time it attributes to religion all the corresponding defects, such as a distorted reflection of reality, contempt of knowledge, hostility to science, passivity and reaction. This undifferentiated view of religion does not do justice to the reality and diversity of the actual existing religions and thus creates a distorted picture more like a caricature than a serious effort to understand the essential nature of religion.

2. Materialistic Atheism narrows Religion down to a Reflection of Reality

One of the most essential elements of the atheistic idea of religion is its view that religion in contrast to science and materialism is a distorted, deformed and fanciful reflection of reality. The implication of this is that the primary function of religion is a rational one of this-worldly objectivity. Of the various roots of religion instanced by atheism obviously the rational root is the most important. Just as in the atheistic view the mind, perception and knowledge have grown and developed, so religion is regarded as a historical category, that has not always existed and so can be overcome. But according to Marx, as against Feuerbach, mind has not only an individual but also a social dimension, and religion is similarly regarded, not only as a private personal matter, but primarily as a collective social affair. In all these aspects, however, religion is primarily interpreted rationally, as a process of the mind and in direct contradiction to reality and is not recognized as being concerned with transcendent supra-rational realities which cannot be derived from matter or from pure immanence.

Materialistic atheism accuses religion primarily of creating a double image of the world or of destroying it, but it overlooks the fact that religion is not the cause of the contradictions and conflicts in the world but only expresses what was already there. Restriction of religion to a rational function and to a distorted reflection of reality rests on the tacit assumption that nature, society and history form a unity, to be brought under one denominator, which can be interpreted purely rationally. Man has an inborn urge to seek a rational understanding of his total experience and a monistic interpretation of existence, and as long as there were and are religions, they remind him that there is not only material nature, not only a world in itself and man in himself, but also other realities, which cannot be understood and explained monistically. The world and existence divided by reason gives an irrational answer, containing 'remainders' which cannot be evenly divided, but which contain the essential and vital part of man's existence, such as conscience, choice and responsibility.

3. *Materialistic Atheism judges Religion from Its Own Anthropocentric Viewpoint*

It is an old experience of mankind that criticism is easier than construction. Therefore it is pertinent in any controversy to ask the participant in view of his sharp criticism how he sees his own position—what has he to offer on his side by way of insights and what standards of value he recognizes. When these questions are applied to the atheistic criticism of religion they receive various answers but all of them are based on one fundamental idea, namely that man is the supreme being. Marx expressed this as early as 1843/4.[1] He never criticised Feuerbach's anthropocentricity, but only his too vague understanding of the idea 'man'. He said that

[1] Marx-Engels, *On Religion*, p. 50.

man was not only part of nature but also a social and producing being. Anthropocentricity is so firmly rooted in materialistic atheism that it became an essential constituent of its philosophy and forms the sole key not only to its understanding of religion, but also to its interpretation of the world and life, and to its understanding of existence and science.

The criticism of religion by materialistic atheism is the counterpart to its positivist interpretation of life and is essentially connected with it. Marx maintains that religion is only the illusory sun which revolves round man, as long as he does not revolve round himself. But he should revolve round himself as his real sun.[1] 'The criticism of religion ends with the doctrine that to man, man is the supreme being.' 'The only liberation of Germany that is possible in practice is liberation on the basis of the theory that regards man as the supreme being.'[2] In this statement the ontological-anthropocentric background of the Marxist criticism of religion is clear.

This strand of anthropocentricity in the criticism of religion, which is also in line with Feuerbach, is found in the early writings of Engels also, primarily in a negative form: 'Religion is essentially the emptying of man and nature of all content, the transfer of this content to the phantom of a supernatural god, who then condescends to grant to men and nature something of his abundance.'[3] According to Engels what happens in religion is that man worships his own being in a different form. Religion is the act of self-evacuation by man and leads to hypocrisy, since it shows men something human and claims that it is something superhuman and divine.[4]

4. *Materialistic Atheism condemns Religion and yet in the End Respects It*

Materialistic atheism recognizes religion as its real opponent, and knows that it is in irreconcilable contrast to it. That is its verdict on religion. It shows some understanding of religion in its early stages of development, at the time of the beginnings of

[1] *Op. cit.*, p. 42.   [2] *Op. cit.*, pp. 50 and 58.
[3] Marx-Engels, *Werke*, vol. 1, Berlin 1956, p. 543.   [4] *Op. cit.*, p. 544.

human society. Here the verdict is still comparatively favourable. But on religion in later times and particularly our own day its attitude is one of criticism and repudiation. More recent writings of materialistic atheism contain frequent condemnation of religion, whereas these give unstinted approval to science, of course as materialistic atheism understands it. In its comparison of science and religion, religion shows up very badly. The following opinion is typical of many others: 'While science gives men a true picture of the world around them, exalts man and makes him strong and powerful, capable of transforming nature and society, religion, which distorts the image of the world, confuses him, dulls his intelligence, transforms him into a miserable slave of nature and social environment. Like opium, religion poisons and deadens the social consciousness of the people, diverts men from their true destiny.'[1]

Marx, Engels and Lenin and most of the more recent atheistic writers have expressed themselves very forcibly against religion, its failure and the harm it does in all spheres of human life and culture. Religion, they say, fails theoretically by providing a false view of the world, and practically by inhibiting action. Its failure in the eyes of materialistic atheism is in relation to the intellectual-rational and practical-ethical sphere of existence. Indeed it is said definitely to glorify ignorance and weakness. There is no fault, no defect, no vice and no crime that is not attributed to religion by materialistic atheism. It would be an onerous but interesting undertaking some time to collect from the atheistic literature of the last hundred years all the accusations levelled against religion. It would yield a long list of faults, a comprehensive catalogue of crimes, a mass of accusations, mostly groundless, but also occasionally justifiable.

And yet the atheistic writers, specially of recent years, are too often guilty of a one-sided and blinkered view of religion. Religion has in fact not only made mistakes and caused misery, but has also done a great deal of good. This good, even in the purely mundane sphere, is overlooked or denied by atheistic writers, and that leads of course to a false overall estimate of religion and over-simplifies

---

[1] Oleshchuk, 'Wissenschaft und Religion', *SUP*, 1954/100.

its refutation. An unjust and false condemnation of religion raises new problems and difficulties. At the same time materialistic atheism both past and present contains within itself possibilities of arriving at an objective verdict about religion, for example in its recognition of the human right to 'freedom of belief and conscience' and its refusal of a ban on religion, in the principle of respect for religious feelings. Although Marx, Engels and Lenin may have been convinced of the alleged falsity and immorality of religion, yet they again and again opposed any general prohibition of it, and that is all the more remarkable, since in their day such demands were frequently made. Whether this opposition to a ban arose from humanistic, liberal or atheistic reasons (a ban would be a stimulus to religion!), its ultimate effect was positive, for within the sphere of influence of materialistic atheism, religion was given the possibility of survival and revival and the opportunity to serve with its own intrinsic power.

Engels expressly rejects the 'abolition of God', which was decided on in 1793 by the extremists during the French Revolution, for he maintained that an enormous number of things can be ordered on paper, without the necessity of carrying them out, and that persecution was the best means of encouraging objectionable beliefs.[1] On another occasion Engels rejected a ban on religion, in opposition to Eugen Dühring,[2] because it would turn religion into martyrdom and prolong its life.[3] Similarly Lenin declined to proclaim a war against religion as a political task of the workers' party. He maintained that the party should work patiently for religion to die out through the organization and education of the proletariat. They should not rush into the adventure of a political crusade against religion. A declaration of war on religion, he said, would be the best way to revive interest in it, and to prevent it from dying out.[4]

Lenin also said definitely that both he and the party were unconditionally opposed to any interference with the religious convictions of all workers who had still retained a belief in God.[5]

---

[1] Marx-Engels, *On Religion*, p. 142.
[2] Philosopher and economist, 1833-1921, who opposed Christianity and Judaism.
[3] *Op. cit.*, p. 148.　　　　[4] Lenin, *Religion*, p. 16f.　　　　[5] *Op. cit.*, p. 22.

5. Religion confronts Atheism with a Serious Problem

Marx and Engels considered religion to be refuted in theory and immoral in practice. Engels too maintained that the scientific view of the world left no room for a creator and ruler of the world, and that true understanding of the forces of nature drives the gods or God out of one position after another, and this process has now gone so far that it may be regarded as concluded.[1]

Thus to Marx and Engels the falsity of religion was proved, and so it was to them only a matter of time before religion would come to its natural end.

However, religion did not come to an end: it is still very much alive. The more recent materialistic atheists are now realistic enough to admit the existence of religion in our day and to ask themselves the correspondingly relevant questions: How is it that religion continues, even though it is rooted in ignorance and in spite of the advance of science? Why is it that, after the social ground has been cut from under its feet in many lands, religion still lives on there? These and other questions are being increasingly heeded by the theorists of materialistic atheism. At the same time it seems that they have not yet faced the fundamental question raised by religion, but are attempting to work out new explanations and theories, which will somehow retain the principles of materialistic atheism and at the same time face the vitality of religion.

Statements that have recently appeared about the 'tough vitality' and 'capacity for adaptation' of religion are examples of such expedient theories, which are supposed to create a balance between the fundamental atheistic view of the roots of religion and a realistic view of the facts. It is even admitted that there is a revival and expansion of religion, and it is gradually dawning on materialistic atheism that religion is not concerned only with the intellectual side of man's nature, but also his emotions and will, and thus claims the whole man, intellect, emotions, will and all.[2]

Within the framework of their own theory of religion present-day atheists attempt to discover the reasons for its persistence and revival. A monograph written in 1958 states: 'As human society

[1] Marx-Engels, *On Religion*, p. 150.   [2] Scheler, *Die Stellung*, p. 5f.

EAG

has not yet completely overcome its dependence on the elementary forces of nature, this dependence can continue to exert a distorting influence on the social consciousness. It must not be forgotten what effects periods of drought, cloudbursts and floods, earthquakes and tornados still exercise on the economy and on human life.'[1] The author of these lines points out with Lenin that war produces terror and despair, with a consequent 'strengthening of religion'. The second world war provided richer nourishment for mysticism and religion than the first.

These realistic insights of materialistic atheism with regard to the survival of religion have of course not been without influence on the atheistic theory of religion. The question here at issue is whether the principle that the economic situation (the economic basis) determines the ideological consciousness (the ideal superstructure) is scientifically demonstrable and universally operative. Is it really true that the method of production ultimately determines also 'religious ideas'? Marx has already written that it is much easier to find by analysis the material kernel of religious illusions than *vice versa* to work out from any actual living conditions their sublimated forms.[2] At the end of his life Engels spoke of the 'ideological realms of philosophy and religion floating still higher in the air', implying that both these realms were further removed from economics than, say, law, politics, education and literature. The historic period had preserved as a legacy from the prehistoric period a great deal of what would today (1890) be called nonsense. The various erroneous ideas about nature, spirits, magic, etc. had only negatively an economic factor as basis, and 'it would be pedantic to try to find economic causes for all this primitive nonsense'.[3]

So even in theory it has not been so very easy to prove the dependence of religious ideas on economic conditions. Marx and Engels both felt this and it is often repeated today: 'Of course the connection between a religious idea and its material basis is particularly difficult to discover and to prove.'[4]

---

[1] Cherkashkin, *Über die sozialen Wurzeln der Religion.*
[2] Marx-Engels, *On Religion*, p. 136.   [3] *Op. cit.*, p. 282.
[4] Scheler, *Die Stellung*, p. 12.

For this reason these religio-historical assertions on the part of materialistic atheism, which deduce the actual development of religion from the economic, social and political conditions have been largely disregarded: they are untenable. The assertion once made by Franz Mehring[1] that in the most important periods of Christianity religious ideas were everywhere dependent on the then existing process of production,[2] cannot be substantiated. Nor would the actual history of the individual religions support Engels' opinion that without the one king there would not have been the one God.[3]

In his essay, 'Early Roots of Religion' Ulrich Seemann tried to construct a historical survey of the relations between the social development of man and the development of the idea of God, from the standpoint of materialistic atheism.[4] In proportion as society gradually split into classes, he thinks, the gods took the form of man-like beings. Whereas at the end of the period of primitive community the multiplicity of gods, like the people, existed side by side as equals, as society split into classes the world of gods was correspondingly rearranged into a hierarchy. At last on the model of the great tyrants in the slave states the idea of one single all-powerful god arose. Thus monotheism arose first in the national religions and then with the formation of great empires it developed into the great monotheistic world religions. 'So the Christian religion arose in the West, out of the various religious ideas current there, with its one almighty, omniscient, all-controlling God, as the reflection of the social conditions, i.e. primarily the class structure of the Roman Empire, which to men of that time in the West was identical with the world.' Seemann sums up the result in this way: 'These changes in man's conception of God are thus only the reflection of human ideas, which were ultimately based on the development of the means of production.'

Seemann's theory is at first sight attractive, but proves to be illogical and unrealistic. According to his logic the classless primitive

---

[1] Politician and author, 1846-1919.
[2] Mehring, *Der historische Materialismus*, p. 100.
[3] Scheler, *Die Stellung*, p. 12.
[4] Seemann, 'Frühe Wurzeln der Religion', *Neues Deutschland*, 6/12/58.

society should have produced henotheism[1] or monotheism,[2] and the class society polytheism, which it did not do. Moreover in actual fact in many individual religions henotheism and monotheism did not originate 'on the model of the great tyrants', but earlier, in the religions of Israel for example. Finally in the national religions henotheism should have developed first, not monotheism. The theory put forward by Seemann, which explains the development of religion from the rise of social and political structures, may be an interesting invention, but it breaks down on the actual history of individual religions.

It is remarkable that Seemann revived this Hegel-like theory in 1958, in view of the fact that as long ago as 1882 Friedrich Engels, arguing from the nature of Christianity, had treated more profoundly and convincingly the development of Christianity into a world religion: 'Since Christianity rejects all national religions and their ritual and appeals to all peoples without distinction, it possesses the possibility of becoming the first universal religion... By expressing clearly the feeling that men are themselves to blame for the general corruption as the guilt of each individual, and by providing in the sacrifice of its judge an easily understood form of the longed-for deliverance, Christianity preserved its capacity to become a world religion, and indeed one peculiarly suited to the existing world.'[3]

Thus it is not so easy to explain the actual development of the various religions on the basis of the idea of religion held by materialistic atheism, for the religions have developed more independently of their economic social and political environment than is admitted by the atheistic theories. It is to the credit of historical materialism to have drawn attention to the existence of economic influences on ideological-religious ideas, but it is not possible to explain directly from economic causes the existence, the form at any particular time, and the overall development of the individual religions, and to do so is to ignore their originality and particularity. And then inevitably one comes across the figure of Jesus Christ, who

---

[1] Belief in one God supreme over all other gods.
[2] Belief in one single God.
[3] Marx-Engels, *On Religion*, pp. 202 and 203.

signifies the end of religion and the beginning of the Gospel in the world.

6. *The Gospel and Religion*

The Gospel is not affected by the theoretical criticism and refutation of religion by materialistic atheism. It stands or falls with the person of Jesus Christ and the Bible, which is his witness. Jesus' testimony to himself, such sayings as 'I am the Way and the Truth and the Life' (John 14.6) cannot be derived from any general concept of religion, but are autonomous statements only valid with regard to one person, Jesus. The only possible attitude to religion consistent with the Gospel is a dialectical one, neither an absolute negative nor an absolute positive. A faith conformed to the Gospel can only see in the other religions the longing, the need for deliverance, without the salvation offered by Jesus Christ in the form he laid down: 'No man cometh unto the Father but by me' (John 14.6).

From this standpoint the theory of religion put forward by materialistic atheism must be allowed some degree of validity, when it sees in religion the work of human hands. Although it is very difficult to assess theoretically or practically the influence of human factors on religion, this influence certainly exists. But even if this questionable generalization is taken into consideration, religion always possesses one permanent function: it points beyond the material-immanent, beyond the mundane-secular.

This poses a lot of preliminary questions to present-day materialistic atheism. Is religion only a reflection of the real world in the mind? Can it not have inferential knowledge of a reality beyond reason? Is religion actually only the expression of curable misery, and at the same time a protest against it? Can it not also be an indication of suffering that it is not in human power to overcome, like sorrow, guilt or death? Religion survives on the hard but necessary insight that there are many things in human life that cannot be explained by science or economics, and that we are individually and collectively subject to limitations both subjective and objective with regard to understanding, knowledge and power to control. On the other hand religion must recognize that it is often possible for men to demonstrate a theory by practice, or in the scientific field by experiments repeatable at will within certain limits. At the same time religion reminds us that in personal and social life there are a lot of processes that are atypical, original and unrepeatable, demanding existential decisions, personal ventures and transcendental responsibility.

It cannot be maintained as a generalization that religion inhibits activity and encourages passivity. The various concrete religions differ too widely in structure for that to be true. Possibly the oriental religions, for example, do particularly encourage contemplation, but another world religion, Islam, demands from its followers the greatest activity. But for the same reason a general judgment on the theory of religion put forward by materialistic atheism cannot be made either. It has to be argued in reference to individual cases. An example may make this clear. Horst Ullrich writes: 'Religion subordinates natural and social development and man himself to a supernatural power (God). By its demands that man must let himself be guided in all his actions by the will and by the commandments of God, it makes him a slave of a power outside the world, upon which he has no influence at all, and to which he is completely subjected. By the precepts of religion man is deprived of the capacity, indeed is expressly forbidden, to be an independent and conscious architect of his social life. The course of his life, like the course of history, is prescribed according to his religious conception of God.'[1]

Each one of these statements would have to be checked by reference to the Gospel. Then Ullrich's complete misunderstanding of religion would become clear, and more particularly of the biblical message. In the sphere of religion alone things are not as simple as Ullrich assumes, but the Gospel demands a quite different approach from the one suggested. Thus the question of religion can in the first instance be left in suspension. The decision is not concerned with this, but with the Bible and the person of Jesus Christ.

[1] Horst Ullrich, 'Der dialektische Materialismus ist unvereinbar mit religiösem Glauben', *Neues Deutschland*, 29/3/58.

3 · Materialistic Atheism on the Bible

PRESENT-DAY MATERIALISTIC ATHEISM TAKES A GREAT interest in the Bible, and for polemical rather than objective reasons. The Bible is not taken seriously for its own sake, but in order to refute it, together with the Christian faith and 'religion'. The Bible is summoned before the tribunal of materialistic atheism and criticized from that position. In the process it may occasionally happen that some sentences in it are assessed positively, but on the whole the verdict is negative.

Friedrich Engels on the Bible and the Revelation of St John

The Bible was of great importance in the intellectual development of Friedrich Engels, not only at first, when he was living in Wuppertal in the atmosphere of pietist Christianity, but also after he had turned away from Christianity under the influence of the 'young Hegelians'. When faith weakens, the Bible loses its spiritual authority as the source and support of faith, and *vice versa*. Some of Engels' statements about the Bible reflect his inner development.

In the first book in which Engels applied the principle of 'historical materialism' to a section of concrete history, *The Peasant War in Germany* (*Der deutsche Bauernkrieg*, 1851), he did not dispute that the Bible described the simple Christianity of the first century, in contrast to the feudalized Christianity of the sixteenth century, but on the other hand he remarked, supporting Thomas Münzer: 'He rejected the Bible both as the exclusive and

as infallible revelation. The real living revelation is reason, a
revelation that has existed at all times and among all peoples and
which still exists. To set reason over against the Bible is to kill the
spirit with the letter, for the Holy Spirit of which the Bible speaks
is not something existing outside us: the Holy Spirit is simply the
reason.'[1] These statements mark a momentous decision on the
problem of the Bible, revelation and reason. According to Engels,
the result of this decision is to regard the Bible as not authoritative
and Jesus as a mere man.

This touches the profoundest questions concerning the Church
and the Christian faith, and reveals the close connection between
the question of the authority of the Bible in the matter of faith and
that of the spiritual authority of Jesus. Basically Engels has here
completely broken with the Bible and with Christ and opened the
way for a purely secular view of the Bible. In 1853 Engels wrote to
Marx that it was now absolutely clear to him that the Jewish so-
called sacred scriptures were no more than the record of the old
Arabian religious and tribal tradition: 'The supposed genealogy of
Noah, Abraham and the rest given in Genesis is a fairly exact
enumeration of the then existing Bedouin tribes according to their
wider or narrower linguistic relations.'[2]

However instructive Engels' agreement with Münzer may be,
his statement about Genesis is equally unimportant. In his later
years Engels turned his attention even more intensively to the
Bible, particularly to the Revelation of St John. But even this
concern with the last book of the Bible did not arise from any
objective interest, but as part of the attempt to refute the Bible
and Christianity and so to justify finally the atheistic position. For
in his three intensive studies of the Book of Revelation between
1882 and 1894 Engels' aim is to contest the historicity of Jesus and
the credibility of the Gospels. These two subjects are indeed still
burning questions today. In the evangelical theology of the
nineteenth century these questions, posed by Bruno Bauer (1809-
1882) and taken up by Friedrich Engels, found no final unequivocal
and convincing answer. They are still being discussed today in a

---

[1] Marx-Engels, *On Religion*, p. 110.
[2] Marx-Engels, *Selected Correspondence*, No. 28, p. 95.

less crude and more clarified form in evangelical theological circles, but they have long since been extended beyond the sphere of theology. Engels' answer to both questions enjoys the highest esteem in present-day materialistic atheism. Disregarding the answers of Bauer and Engels, as historically untenable and philosophically out of date, it is a sign of vitality that the questions about the historicity of Jesus and the credibility of the Gospels have again come to the fore. For this reason alone Engels' theories about the Book of Revelation deserve consideration.

Engels' preoccupation with the Revelation of St John and the rise of Christianity produced three literary results: *Bruno Bauer and Primitive Christianity* (*Bruno Bauer und das Urchristentum*, 1882), *The Book of Revelation* (*Das Buch der Offenbarung*, 1883) and *On the History of Primitive Christianity* (*Zur Geschichte des Urchristentums*, 1894-5). The theories there put forward about the Bible and Christianity are still largely maintained by materialistic atheism and are propagated particularly in popular scientific literature.[1]

Engels' works on the Bible and Christianity are not based on his own research,[2] but relied mostly on Bruno Bauer, whom he himself at first had called a 'literary crank'. Later on he dissociated himself more strongly from him.[3]

Bruno Bauer started out originally as a right-wing Hegelian. He reduced first the Gospel of John and then the synoptics to the product of mystical fancy and denied them any historical basis. Jesus had only made religion, the self-consciousness of the personality, clearer to the world. Meanwhile Bauer had completely abandoned Christianity and reached the standpoint of pure immanence and atheism. Christianity seemed to him at last only a rejection of the world, whereas true self-consciousness recognized

[1] Three articles by Engels in: Marx-Engels, *On Religion*, pp. 193, 204, and 313. Almost all the more recent statements by materialistic atheism about Christianity (origin, nature, and the Revelation of St John) have taken over Engels' theses as proven (Mashkin, Mishulin, and the Textbooks for History Teaching in the 5th and 9th school years). Only the Textbook for the 9th school year (2nd edition 1953, p. 277) deviates from the year AD 68 as the date of the book of Revelation. Heinrich Fuchss (*Hat die Bibel recht?*) adheres to 'the year 68 of our era', but puts the epistles of St Paul between 53 and 63 and the Gospels 'about 70', considerably earlier than Engels.
[2] Marx-Engels, *On Religion*, pp. 194 and 321.
[3] *Op. cit.*, pp. 197 and 321f.

nature and its laws. It is interesting that Bauer's feelings of hatred against theology developed parallel with his conservatism. Since 1850 he had declared the figure of Jesus to be unhistorical, the product of mystical fancy. At the same time against all historical evidence he set the epistles of St Paul in the second century AD. In the seventies he turned his attention to the rise of Christianity, which he professed to be able to explain from the stoicism of Seneca (4 BC-AD 65) and the Judaism of Philo (25 BC-AD 40). These basic principles of Bauer's hypotheses occur again in Engels' three books.

In line with Bauer Engels maintained that the Book of Revelation was the oldest book in the New Testament, belonging to the very earliest period of Christianity. He placed the Acts and Pauline epistles, at least in their present form, sixty years later than Revelation. The Gospels and the Acts he considered to be later recensions of lost manuscripts. Thus Revelation is the only book in the New Testament which can be really accurately dated within a few months. In his view it must have been written between June 67 and January or April 68, and consequently there is no doubt that Revelation with its exceptionally authenticated date was the oldest book of all Christian literature.

Engels further maintains that Revelation is not only the oldest book of the New Testament, but the only one whose genuineness cannot be doubted. John was a Jew, he says, which is quite clear from his many Hebraisms and bad Greek. He was 'neurotic' but at the same time much respected amongst the Christians of Asia Minor. But John had borrowed all the material of his book, thus showing a quite unusual poverty of mind. Consequently the trances and visions he describes were not even the experiences of his own imagination. Engels further maintains that the Gospel, the Epistles and Revelation had at least three different authors. Revelation demonstrably did not originate from the same writer as the Gospel or the Epistles of St John. In the way described in Revelation Christianity had been created in Asia Minor, its main centre, about the year 68.

The value of Revelation is seen by Engels in the fact that it is the simplest and clearest book of the New Testament and not the most obscure and mysterious. Thanks to modern German biblical criticism it has become the most easily understood and the clearest. For in reading Revelation it is possible to get an idea of how Christianity looked in its earliest form. Here we have Christianity in the most primitive form that has been preserved for us. As an authentic picture of primitive Christianity Revelation is more valuable than all the rest of the books of the New Testament together. It is thus specially valuable, because it shows what Judaism has contributed to Christianity.

Engels considers the struggle between God and Antichrist as described in chapters 13 and 17 to be a vital part of Revelation. The prophecies of subsequent events have lost all significance, except for such simple people as still try to calculate the date of the last judgment. In Revelation the primary role is played by an uncritical mixture of the grossest superstitions—miracle, trance, visions, spirits, prophecy, alchemy, occult lore and other magical nonsense. It was in this atmosphere that the Church had its origin.

Engels' Theories about Revelation are adopted and repeated with Some Caution

Engels regarded the figure of Jesus in the Book of Revelation, the assumed oldest book in the New Testament, as so mythical and unhistorical, so glorified and unreal, that the book provided the strongest support for his thesis of the unhistoricity of Jesus. He seems to believe that at first there had existed a mythical picture of Jesus (i.e. in Revelation) and then this hazy mythical figure had been given real historical features (in the Gospel) and had become a part of history. This explanation is extraordinary and tendentious and cannot be sustained in face of the internal evidence of the New Testament writings and the history of the New Testament canon. The normal view of the origin of the New Testament books, confirmed by research and according to which Revelation is not dated at the beginning but at the end of the books, destroys the whole structure of Bauer's and Engel's theory. Since the end of the nineteenth century a whole series of discoveries have been made and new knowledge gained, which refute finally Engels' dating of the New Testament books.

Engels' theories about Revelation, which influence his view of the Gospels, have been taken up again and circulated in the statements of modern materialistic atheism about the New Testament canon. Mashkin in his *Roman History* (*Römische Geschichte*, Berlin 1953) adopts Engels' order of the origin of the New Testament books: Revelation, Epistles, Gospels, Acts. Mashkin asserts that one of the earliest Christian literary monuments is the Revelation of St John, which had been written at the end of the year 68 or the beginning of 69, during the Civil War and after the death of Nero. The translator of Mashkin's work had recognized Engels' earlier date 67/8 as a printers' error and corrected it in Mashkin to 68/9.[1]

The *Textbook for History Teaching in the Ninth School Year*[2] (*Lehrbuch für den Geschichtsunterricht*, 9. *Schuljahr*, 1952) states that the Revelation of John 'was written towards the end of the year 67 or the beginning of 68 during the Civil War and after the death of Nero'.[3] Here too Engels' order of the New Testament writings is retained. An analysis of this account shows that the statements of the textbook are a combination of Engels' dating of Revelation (erroneously as 67/8 instead of 68/9) with Mashkin's more detailed assertion 'during the Civil War and after the death of Nero'. In the 1953 edition the textbook altered the date of Revelation from Nero's time to about 30 years later, namely to the reign of Domitian (AD 81-96). Engels' date has been abandoned but his chronology of the books of the New Testament has not been corrected. Revelation is still said to be the oldest of the New Testament books.[4]

The Revelation of St John, according to the present state of knowledge, was actually written not in Nero's reign, but at the time of Domitian. The discovery of the Gallio inscription (1931) places the date of St Paul's two Epistles to the Thessalonians in the year 51/52 and proves them, and not Revelation, to be the oldest books in the New Testament. The discovery in Engels'

[1] N. A. Mashkin, *Römische Geschichte*, pp. 549-51.
[2] History textbook in use in the East German Republic.
[3] *Lehrbuch für den Geschichtsunterricht*, 9. *Schuljahr*, Part 4, Berlin 1952, p. 76.
[4] *Ibid.*, p. 277 (ed. 1953).

lifetime, of the oldest New Testament manuscript, the Codex Sinaiticus, by Konstantin von Tischendorf (1859) also shows that the Revelation of St John originated at the end of the New Testament period. The history of the establishment of the canon of the New Testament shows that Revelation was the book in most dispute and was not the first to be written but the last. For all these reasons Revelation does not belong to the early period, but the late period of the formation of the New Testament canon. The collapse of the theory that Revelation is the oldest book of the New Testament drags with it the statements dependent on it. Furthermore the question of the historicity of Jesus can be answered in a better way, because freer from prejudice, than was the case at the end of the nineteenth century with the then available knowledge.

The Bible in the View of Historical Materialists

Engels' criticism of the Bible was based primarily on reason and history. We can trace also the beginnings of a criticism based on materialistic sociology, but this was developed particularly by Kautsky and Mehring. Karl Kautsky (1854-1938) wrote of the Bible: 'This book is the result of the most diverse social conditions and tendencies, from barbaric gentile society to the society of imperial Rome, which reached the highest level of simple economic production, and which collapsed on the threshold of capitalistic production. Up to the time of the domination of capitalistic means of production there was no class or party which did not find in the Bible its own patterns and arguments.'[1]

What Kautsky has written here is in a sense correct. The expanse of time covered by the Bible extends from the creation of the world through the middle of time with the incarnation of Jesus Christ to his second coming on the last day. The period of the composition of the Bible from its beginning to its completion extends over a thousand years, and so it is only to be expected that it reflects the most diverse social, cultural and political conditions and developments. The fact that the most diverse parties and movements appeal to the Bible is nothing against it, but is a clear indication

[1] Mehring, *Über historischen Materialismus*, p. 102.

that it possesses its own authority at all the many levels, and that men readily make use of this. For even a book like the Bible is not proof against misuse. Jesus occasionally quoted passages from the Old Testament scriptures, but so did the evil spirit who tried to tempt the Son of God to disobedience and apostasy (Matt. 4.6). But the Bible challenges every man to seek out its real content and fundamental meaning.

Franz Mehring developed Kautsky's idea further, but in doing so made it unacceptable by finding the reason for the Bible's great influence in its contradictions: 'The fact that the Bible was the book of books for the European peoples for more than a thousand years, and that it exerted a unique influence on the intellectual and religious life of these peoples, was not because of its divine and incontestable truth, but just because of its numerous contradictions.'[1]

Kautsky and Mehring's verdict on the Bible remains completely superficial and does not understand its real nature. But there are other voices from the sphere of materialistic atheism which are fairer to the Bible, or to some parts of it.

The Bible finds a Certain Social Recognition

Not only in the history of primitive Christianity, but also in the Bible, there are some parts that find acceptance with materialistic atheism. Among them is the social implication discernible in the utterances of the Prophets of Israel and in the teaching of Jesus. The loving words of Jesus to the 'weary and heavy laden' found an echo in materialistic atheism from the time of Engels to the present, a sign that acts and words of genuine mercy in the name of God are rewarding in the atheistic milieu also, and that intolerance can make nonsense of the cause of the people of God.

It is nevertheless remarkable to read in a Soviet *Textbook of the History of the Ancient East* (*Lehrbuch über die Geschichte des alten Orients*) for use in state universities and educational institutes: 'In the books of the Prophets, since the second half of the eighth century BC, there are sharp accusations against the rich, who lived in luxury and enriched themselves at the expense of the poor.

[1] Mehring, *Über historischen Materialismus*, p. 102.

The prophets, who were close to the unofficial priesthood, largely associated with the mass of the middle section of the population, attacked the grievous exploitation of the poor by the rich. The prophets Amos, Micah and Isaiah criticized particularly harshly the greedy rich, who were continually trying to enrich themselves at the expense of the poorest section of the population.' The author of the *Textbook*, W. J. Avdiyev, refers particularly to Amos 8.5-8 and sums up: 'The Prophets, who attacked the rich who were living in wealth and luxury and striving for personal enrichment, fought for the return to the earlier patriarchal tribal life. However, these attempts to arrest the process of economic development and the disruption of the free peasantry could not achieve any tangible results.'[1] Intense interest in the Bible and the recognition of its social principles is likewise to be found in a book by Ernst Bloch, *The Hope Principle (Das Prinzip Hoffnung)*. In volume two he has an outline on social utopias, which gives a prominent place to the biblical statements. Ernst Bloch (b. 8th July, 1885) can, of course, hardly be definitely classed as a materialistic atheist and is not recognized by present day atheism, but his philosophy is predominantly rooted in materialistic ideas, so that his verdict on the Bible is not out of place here. At the Conference on Bloch's Philosophy at the beginning of April 1957 his philosophy was charged with being a revision of Marxism, and a year later Manfred Buhr attempted to show that Ernst Bloch's hope-philosophy had its origin in religion, specifically in the Revelation of St John, and in the book of Exodus.[2] Its ultimate significance is the effort to maintain religion and so to reconcile religion and Marxism, and to express religious ideas in Marxist terminology.

In his comprehensive work Bloch writes also on *The Bible and the Implication of loving One's Neighbour (Bibel und Reich der Nächstenliebe)*. He begins with a historical section, actually with Moses, to whom God was a God of deliverance, a God of exodus from slavery: 'This exodus gives the Bible from thenceforth a keynote which it has never lost, and there is no book in which the

[1] Avdiyev, *Geschichte des alten Orients*, p. 319.
[2] *Ernst Blochs Revision des Marxismus*, Berlin 1957; Manfred Buhr, 'Der religiöse Ursprung und Charakter der Hoffnungsphilosophie Ernst Blochs', *Deutsche Zeitschrift für Philosophie*, 1958/4/576ff.

memory of nomadic social organization, still half communistic, has endured so powerfully as in the Bible.' 'In the midst of the exploitation during the early Israelite kingdom, especially under Solomon, the Prophets appeared, fulminating against it, and set forth a system of justice, which is at the same time the oldest ground plan of a social utopia.' Bloch mentions the Nazarites (Numbers 6) and the Rechabites (II Kings 10.15 and Jer. 35.14ff). They, Samson, Samuel, Elijah and John the Baptist, were enemies of the golden calf and the luxurious dominant church. 'From the semi-primitive communism of Nazarite memory to the preaching of the Prophets against wealth and tyranny, and on to the early Christian communism of love, there is a single recognizable interwoven thread. It forms an almost unbroken *leitmotif* and the familiar prophetic pictures of the future state of social peace take their colour from a golden age that had become only a legend.'[1] Amos is singled out by Avdiyev and approved, as also by Bloch. Isaiah, Deutero-Isaiah and Micah are also praised. Jesus himself, Bloch further maintains, was not so completely and exclusively concerned with the individual and with the next world as the Pauline reinterpretation, biassed in favour of the ruling class, would make out. The great 'Logion' in Matt. 11.25-30 (the 'Saviour's call') referred to this world, not the next, and was a proclamation of the Messiah-King, who would put an end to suffering in every form, here on earth, as one to whom all things had been delivered to be transformed. 'The Bible has not set out a social utopia, and that is not its main purpose or its ultimate value. To believe that would be falsely to estimate the Bible and stupid at the same time. Christianity is not just an outcry against death and futility, and brings into both the Son of Man. But although the Bible contains no detailed social utopia, it points most definitely, in negation and also in affirmation, towards this Exodus and this Kingdom.'[2]

The Bible is Recognized as Having some Cultural Significance

To Christians the Bible is first and foremost a witness to and record of the great acts of God in Christ. The richness of the

---

[1] Ernst Bloch, *Das Prinzip Hoffnung*, vol. 2, Berlin 1955, p. 58f.
[2] *Op. cit.*, pp. 61 and 63.

human spirit provides other points of view from which to regard
the Bible. To the non-Christian it will be at best a monument to
the literature and culture of the past. In this sense there are voices
from the field of materialistic atheism that at least allow the Bible
a certain cultural significance. In one case the translation of the
Hebrew literature into all the European languages is acknowledged
to have exercised a powerful influence.[1]

There is a still more positive view of the Bible in a book dated
1949 on the Danish poet Martin Andersen Nexö: 'The Bible, this
compendium of Jewish literature, impressed with the new idea
of the one God as the creator of the world and the Father of all
men, is the most powerful work of world literature ever. Not only
is the older part the book of devotion and of law for the Jews, but
together with the later part this Christian book of books has been
translated into all the languages in the world and circulated in
thousands of millions of copies. Most European literatures
began with translations, commentaries and paraphrases of the
Bible. The Psalms form a permanent constituent of the catholic
liturgy and are the models for the hymns of all the Christian
peoples. Countless biblical stories and figures have been handed
down as oral legends: they have appeared hundreds and hundreds
of times in the literature of Christian countries. Books about the
Bible form an enormous literature, filling vast libraries. The style
of the Bible has exercised a lasting influence on the poetry and prose
of all peoples. In the process thousands of details have passed into
daily use as expressions and images. Towns, churches, squares,
streets and people bear biblical names. There is no single work
existing which has comprehensively and exactly gathered all this
material together. If it were available and its contents generally
familiar, fanatical race persecutions would scarcely have become
widespread. How is it possible to wish to eradicate something which
is such an integral part of the background of one's own life, however
far one may have moved away from it?'[2]

Materialistic atheism has moreover recognized the importance

[1] *Lehrbuch für den Geschichtsunterricht, 9. Schuljahr*, Part 3, Berlin 1951,
p. 23; also the editions of 1953, 1954 and 1955, p. 117.
[2] Walter A. Berendsohn, *Martin Andersen Nexös Weg in die Weltliteratur*,
Berlin 1949, p. 20.

of Luther's translation of the Bible and has studied its effect in various directions. In the *Textbook for History Teaching in the Sixth School Year (Lehrbuch für Geschichtsunterricht, 6. Schuljahr)*, 1951-55 editions, Luther's contribution to the development of the German language is acknowledged: 'The great merit of Luther is that he contributed to the creation of a uniform German language; for Luther's Bible was soon read throughout Germany. This uniform German language helped to maintain the belief in the unity of Germany, even in the time of division into different states under their own princes.'[1] Also in the new textbook for History teaching in the sixth school year, *Peasants, Townsmen and Feudal Lords (Bauern, Bürger und Feudalherren)*, Berlin, 1957, Luther's translation of the Bible is given a detailed and favourable account and its contribution to the history of the German language acknowledged: 'Luther's translation of the Bible contributed to creating a unified German language out of the dialects of the different regions.[2] In the *Textbook for History Teaching in the Tenth School Year*, 1954-6 editions, it says: 'Although some twenty translations of the Bible had existed before Luther, it was Luther's Bible particularly that became a sharp sword in the hands of the people in their fight against feudalism. The unified German language, however, in the development of which Luther played such an outstanding part, was a strong bond, that in spite of the centuries of political division, contributed essentially to maintaining the hope of a unified Germany. The unified German language is one of the elements in the German nation.'[3]

The recognition of the Bible by materialistic atheism in a social, cultural and linguistic respect, is welcome and not to be underestimated, even though it does not say the last word as to its real meaning as the witness to God's word and acts.

[1] *Lehrbuch für den Geschichtsunterricht, 6. Schuljahr*, Part 2, Berlin/Leipzig 1951, p. 105; also the editions of 1953, p. 142, Berlin 1955, p. 118.
[2] *Lehrbuch für den Geschichtsunterricht, 6. Schuljahr (Bauern, Bürger und Feudalherren)*, Berlin 1957, p. 161f.
[3] *Lehrbuch für den Geschichtsunterricht, 10. Schuljahr*, vol. 3, Berlin 1954, p. 30f; *ibid.*, Berlin 1954, p. 244f.

How is the Biblical Criticism of Materialistic Atheism to be judged?

Materialistic atheism did not invent biblical criticism, but took over what already existed and carried it further in its own interest and with its own slant, in order to shake the credibility of the Bible and to contribute towards the destruction of the Christian faith.

The term 'biblical criticism' is not unequivocal, but conceals a variety of motives. In one sense biblical criticism is as old as the Bible itself, and is a necessary starting point for analysis, sifting and sorting. The disputes within the churches about the canon of the Bible (Old Testament, Apocrypha, New Testament) and the value of particular sections of it, stem from informed biblical criticism. An essential part of biblical criticism is the collecting, sifting and evaluation of particular manuscripts, in order as far as possible to arrive at the oldest and most reliable texts and thus to convey the actual words of Jesus. In this sense biblical criticism is a valid task of the Church, which never reaches finality, although the theological work of the last few decades particularly has attained astonishingly positive results. Such a mighty book as the Bible reflects of course the most diverse stages of human development and because the Word has become flesh and the witnesses to God's great acts in Christ were also subject to literary contingencies, the Bible is subject to the categories of literary criticism. But this can be regarded just as preliminary work, which only reveals the real questions: What authoritative word does the Bible speak about God and Christ, about us and the world in which we live? To that extent it is more than and different from literature and culture and has permanent existential significance.

The term 'biblical criticism' can also mean destructive criticism, the efforts to discredit the Bible, to pull it to pieces and bring it into contempt in every possible way, with the object of disputing the majesty of God and the incarnation of Jesus Christ to which the Bible testifies. There was actually a pamphlet once entitled: 'The great horror—the Bible not the word of God!' That is indeed the question—whether it is the word of God or not; and the answer to this question goes far beyond the scope of mere literature, and demands responsible personal decision. This sort of biblical criticism is a product of the eighteenth and nineteenth centuries, and in fact grew up amongst the idealistic and liberal bourgeoisie and not amongst the proletariat at all. This destructive criticism has attacked the Bible on three different grounds, philosophical, historical and scientific. Today, after two hundred years, it can be said that the Bible has withstood the threefold ordeal by fire, and is still fulfilling its special function, to the glory of God and for the salvation of men.

Friedrich Engels once wrote in reference to Christianity: 'A religion that conquered the Roman Empire and dominated the greatest part of the civilized world for 1,800 years cannot be disposed of just by declaring it to be a lot of nonsense concocted by charlatans.'[1] That is equally true of the Bible and its significance in the life of the nations.

The evidence produced by biblical criticism against the Bible from the spheres of philosophy, history and science has however now been taken over by materialistic atheism to support its own aims. This can be illustrated by three recent examples.

The first example relates to the Old Testament. An article on the manuscripts discovered at Qumran says: 'Thus the new discoveries show that the history of the text of the Old Testament does not differ in principle from the history of the text of every other ancient work. That is not surprising, since the Old Testament is a collection of legends and chronicles, which only the imagination of theologians pronounced sacred. This thesis, already long since proved by progressive scientists, has now been confirmed once again by the manuscripts from the caves in the desert of Judea.'[2]

The second example relates to the New Testament and comes from a pamphlet published in 1958: 'What the Church commends to Christians today as "Holy Scriptures" has been shown long ago by scientific biblical critics to be an arbitrary selection from a large number of conflicting writings from early Christian times. The four evangelists lived much later than the legendary Jesus, whose

[1] Marx-Engels, *On Religion*, p. 194.
[2] A. P. Kashdan, 'Handschriften erzählen', *SUP*, 1957/55/1221 (17/5/57).

disciples and apostles they were supposed to have been. Recently a number of manuscripts from Palestine have been deciphered showing that some of the Christian teaching was written down two hundred years before the "birth of Christ". In these circumstances the conclusion is justified that the Christian religion was concocted at the first Council, basically in the interest of the property owners and their state.'[1]

The third example relates to both parts of the Bible and comes from a book by Heinrich Fuchss, *Is the Bible Right?* (*Hat die Bibel recht?*) It states that the opposition of the Church to scientific advance is based on a system that has been applied uniformly through all the centuries: 'It is the dogma that the Holy Scriptures, the Old and the New Testaments, and also the writings of the Church Fathers, are not the work of human hands, but represent a divine revelation, the absolute divine truth, word for word and letter for letter, to doubt which or to alter which is the mortal sin of blasphemy (verbal inspiration).'[2] In his book Fuchss tries to maintain 'that the Holy Scriptures reflect the state of knowledge of a period more than one thousand years before our era and that these writings are influenced by ideas which the ancient Hebrews took over from other oriental nations and developed further. These ideas persisted in the thought of the New Testament.'[3]

Fuchss' book, obviously intended as a reply to Warner Keller's *The Bible as History* [ET, 1956] (*Und die Bibel hat doch recht— Forscher beweisen die historische Wahrheit*)[4] had a considerable success in its day, but provoked criticism also. Representatives of the Church are said to have called it 'a collection of scandal stories', so that the publishers had to defend Fuchss in a footnote to the third edition. In fact Fuchss does not go into the question which is the main title of his book at all, but is more concerned with the sub-title 'a ramble through the history of the conflict between theology and scientific advance'. He tries to demonstrate the obstructive influence of the Bible on every branch of science—the physical sciences, law, meteorology, medicine, astronomy and so on. The charges brought against Christianity from the history of

[1] H. Wessel, *Kreuz und Bundesadler*, Berlin 1958, p. 16.
[2] Heinrich Fuchss, *Hat die Bibel recht?*, Leipzig/Jena 1957, 3rd ed. 1958, p. 11.
[3] *Ibid.*   [4] *Op. cit.*, p. 220.

the Church well deserve to be taken seriously, but as far as the subject itself is concerned, 'Is the Bible right?', the author has been guilty of serious errors, mostly due to inadequate knowledge of his subject. Fuchss mentions fourteen Pauline epistles that were supposed to have been written between 53 and 63, but there are only thirteen in the New Testament. He places mistakenly the Book of Revelation in the year 68, following Bauer and Engels. The Gospels, he says, were composed 'about the year 70'. Here he differs from Bauer and Engels. 'Originally these collections (the New Testament writings) made no claim to validity for use in worship or to canonical authority.'[1] The number of versions and variants of New Testament texts he estimates at over 30,000. 'It must be remembered', he said, 'that the Hebrew language is read backwards, which means that every book begins in the bottom right-hand corner of the last page and ends in the top left-hand corner of the first.'[2] In all these statements about the Bible there are erroneous or distorted opinions.

Fuchss' statements about the relation between the Bible and faith are more important than these misrepresentations in the literary and historical field: 'In studying the biblical text we should not be guided by a blind belief in the truth of every single sentence and word, but our critical faculties should open our eyes so that we can learn to distinguish clearly and soberly between fact and fancy.'[3] The doctrine of the infallibility of the Bible had developed in the Christian Church, due to the Church Fathers, into a rigid hair-splitting body of dogma. While in the Catholic Church the rigidity of belief in the infallibility of the text of the Bible had become modified towards the end of the Middle Ages, the belief in the Bible had reached its zenith in the Protestant churches. Luther set up the authority of the Holy Scriptures in place of the discarded authority of the Pope.[4] The divine authorship of the Holy Scriptures, Fuchss maintains, was a legend, and the human mind makes a grave mistake, if it lets itself be guided by blind belief in so-called supernatural revelation instead of by the light of reason.[5]

---

[1] *Op. cit.*, p. 36.   [2] *Op. cit.*, p. 37.   [3] *Op. cit.*, p. 33f.
[4] *Op. cit.*, p. 43.   [5] *Op. cit.*, p. 48.

The Bible in the Cross-fire of Philosophical, Historical and Scientific
    Criticism

All the objections adduced against the Bible amount to three
fields of criticism, which have developed in this order in the history
of western thought.

'The Bible in the cross-fire of philosophical criticism' might be
the heading of the first group of criticisms. We can include under
this heading the fantastic identification of revelation, reason and
the Holy Spirit, alleged to have been outlined by Münzer and
taken over by Engels, i.e. the attempt to include completely God,
Jesus and the Bible in the purely natural world. The tension
between the word of God and man's, between revelation and
reason, between God and the world, is superficially dissolved
pantheistically, leading ultimately to the Spinozan formula *'deus
sive natura'*—God or nature. Materialistic atheism does not suc-
ceed in completely carrying through this rationalistic-naturalistic
reduction of the Bible and its content to pure this-worldliness,
but has produced instead another rationalistic pattern, the
opposition of the reason to the Bible. For example H. Fuchss puts
the letter, word and revelation of the Bible on one side and reason
on the other. His statements about the relation of Christians to the
Bible are distorted. A little consideration of the creed and the
confessions would make it quite clear that the Christian faith is
not a matter of the letter of the Bible nor the Bible as a whole, but
concerns the triune God, who has revealed himself to men once
and for all through his Son. Thus the Bible is not, as Fuchss
makes out, the object of faith, but the medium and instrument of
the revelation of God.

'The Bible under the cross-fire of historical criticism'—this
might be the heading of the second group of criticisms. The
question here is the simple recognition that the revelation of God
from the creation of the world to the second coming of Jesus
Christ produced a literary deposit in the form of writings, reports
and letters. The acts, words and prayers in the Bible go back to
men whose writings have been subject to the same laws and
accidents as any other literature. The fact that the history of the
text of the Old Testament books does not differ in principle from

the history of any other text was not revealed for the first time by the Qumran discoveries. But from a purely historical point of view it is not true that the Old Testament is nothing more than a collection of legends and chronicles. There is much more in it, as a glance at the contents-list would show: history, stories, poems, prayers, criticism, exhortation, consolations, prophecies, etc. Was it just the imagination of theologians that declared the legends and chronicles sacred? No, the Bible itself claims to bear witness to the holy God, to reveal his will, his power in history and his judgment, and to expose man's disobedience, guilt and rebellion. The human-literary form of the Bible, the historical interweaving of events and persons, are no reproach against its content and the claims of God, but simply confirm that God is Lord of the world and even takes human history seriously, and has made use of, and still makes use of, men whom he chooses.

'The Bible under the cross-fire of scientific criticism'—that might be the heading of the third group of criticisms of the Bible. The Holy Scriptures, says Fuchss, reflect the state of knowledge of a period much more than 1,000 years before our era. This statement is clearly meant to show that the Bible is out of date and no longer authoritative. It is an attempt to undermine the credibility of the individual books of the Bible in the name of a new scientific understanding of the world. But ever since Luther's day it has been realized that the Bible is no textbook of general human knowledge, but is a witness to God's word and acts, offering men salvation through faith in Jesus Christ.

In the meantime Christendom has also learned to distinguish, in the different books of the Bible, between the enduring substance of revelation and the mode of expression conditioned by time and outlook. It is an essential part of the historicity and reality of the biblical testimony to revelation that it was given in accordance with the existing outlook and culture, and not in abstract generalities. 'The word became flesh.'

Thus every generation is faced with the task of examining the witness as conditioned by the outlook of its time and with its original meaning, discovering its compelling claims on us men of today, and finding a responsible answer. It is true that evangelical theology only discovered very late this distinction between the content of revelation and the understanding of the world, and has often thought it necessary to accept the understanding of the world with the witness to the mighty acts of God. The question of the relation between revelation and understanding of the world was not first raised by materialistic atheism; it is much older. During the last twenty years it has been studied afresh by theologians with seriousness and passion.

The Bible has defeated this threefold attack in the fields of philosophy, history and science and will continue to do so. The biblical criticism of earlier centuries, which has been revived again today by materialistic atheism, serves, however, the unintended purpose of bringing the Bible into a focus of attention. Materialistic atheism judges the Bible fragmentarily, from Genesis, the Gospels and the Revelation of St John, and in the process wastes its energies in wholesale condemnation or loses itself in incidental trifles. The favourable recognition of isolated parts, texts or figures of the Bible makes the overall condemnation still more obvious. None of the modern atheistic writers has devoted more attention to the Bible than Engels. There is no longer any attempt made to investigate the essential meaning of the Bible. In general the atheistic writers confine themselves to reviving the earlier criticisms of the Bible that were presented much better in earlier centuries; they do not concern themselves with the internal self-testimony of the Holy Scriptures.

The textual and literary research and verification of the biblical texts has made such progress today that it can be stated with probability bordering on certainty that the text of the Bible, particularly of the New Testament, is known almost in its original form. Luther's attitude to the Bible is generally recognized as being mistaken. In his early days he was obsessed with the knowledge and certainty of salvation revealed in the Bible. In spite of his devotion to the scriptures he was not a 'biblicist' in the sense that he wished to set up the Bible literally as an external legal authority. He found in the Bible the word of God. In 1522 he claimed that the 'right touchstone' is whether the books of the Holy Scripture speak of

Christ (*Christum treiben*) or not. 'Anything that does not tell of
Christ is not apostolic, even though St Peter or St Paul taught it.
On the other hand whatever tells of Christ would be apostolic,
even though Judas, Annas, Pilate or Herod said it.'[1] It was not
individual writings that were authoritative for Luther, but their
content, not their apostolic authorship, but their witness to Christ.

Against the various statements of materialistic atheism about
the Bible it must be urged: 'The Holy Scriptures are the norm, as
being prophetic and apostolic testimony to the Gospel.' 'The
Gospel, as a promise, is at the same time the announcement of the
forgiveness of sins.'[2]

That is the heart of the Gospel, and that is what the Bible is
concerned with. It is not affected by atheistic biblical criticism.
Hence the theological declaration of the confessional synod at
Barmen in 1934 states: 'Jesus Christ, as witnessed to us in the
Holy Scriptures, is the one Word of God that we have to hear,
to trust in life and death, and to obey.'

[1] From the *Introductions to the Epistles to the Hebrews, St James and St Jude*
(Martin Luther's Works revised and edited by Julius Boehmer, Stuttgart,
1907).
[2] Edmund Schlink, *Theologie der lutherischen Bekenntnisschriften*, Berlin
1954, pp. 19 and 36.

4 · Materialistic Atheism on Jesus Christ and Christianity

THE ATHEIST SEEMS TO FEEL IMPEDED IN HIS AUTONOMOUS development by the Bible and its message, and so in his biblical criticism his first concern is to assert that the Bible is out of date and so not authoritative. His attitude to the figure of Jesus Christ points in the same direction. He tries to get rid of him by denying his historicity and his claims.

From Feuerbach to Lenin

Ludwig Feuerbach in his philosophy of religion laid down the fundamental reasons for the attitude of materialistic atheism to the person of Jesus Christ, even if modern atheism does not realize it or has no longer any understanding of the attempted profundity of Feuerbach's thought. In *The Nature of Christianity* Feuerbach writes about 'the mystery of the incarnation, or God as the object of love': 'The consciousness of love is that by which man reconciles himself with God, or rather with himself, his own being, which he sets up against himself in effect as another being. The consciousness of divine love, or what comes to the same thing the view of God as himself a human being, is the mystery of the incarnation— God becoming flesh, or becoming man. The incarnation is nothing else than the actual material manifestation of the human nature of God. As far as he is concerned, God did not become man: necessity, man's own need, which is still the need of the religious mind, was the foundation of the incarnation. God became man out of mercy—so he was already himself a human God before he actually became man, for he felt pity for the human need, for human misery. The incarnation was a tear of divine compassion, i.e. just the manifestation of a being feeling in a human way, and therefore, himself essentially human.'[1]

These words of Feuerbach, although difficult to understand, lead to the conclusion that God himself is the product of human need, an idea that was then taken over and elaborated by Marx in his well-known words about religion. The key to the right understanding of Feuerbach's statements lies in the following thesis: 'This God become man is only the manifestation of man become God, for the condescension of God to man necessarily precedes the rising of man to God.'[2] This statement contains the whole difficulty of Feuerbach's philosophy of religion and the materialistic atheism associated with it. For it raises the specific question whether God is a living person and self-attesting creator and Lord, as the Holy Scriptures testify and Christendom confesses, or whether he is the product of human imagination and need, as idealistic and materialistic atheists, by reason of their definite assumptions and their definite aims, assert.

Feuerbach started from philosophy, specifically from Hegel, and remained in that field to the extent that he tried to resolve history into speculation and historical figures into ideas. For this reason he came to terms with ideas like religion and creation, incarnation and mysticism, but in doing so overlooked specifically historical facts and failed to do justice to the historical figure of Jesus Christ. At the time when Feuerbach, Marx and Engels laid the foundation of materialistic atheism the figure of Jesus Christ did not occupy the central place in the Church that it does today. Rationalism and romanticism tended to regard the insights of reason and the stimulus of emotions more than the encounter with Jesus Christ or the confrontation with the Word of God as the basis of faith. Heinrich Heine observes with biting irony that at that time it was possible to have Christianity without the divinity of Christ, like turtle soup without turtle.[3] It is a matter of shame

---

[1] Feuerbach, *Das Wesen des Christentums*, vol. 1, Berlin 1956, p. 103f.
[2] *Op. cit.*, p. 104.
[3] Heinrich Heine, *Geständnisse* (Works, vol. 14, Hamburg, 1874), p. 298.

rather than surprise that the leading materialistic atheists failed to come to terms with Jesus Christ.

The only statement of the mature Karl Marx about Christ as far as is known, says that what he, Karl Marx, liked best about the Christ of the Bible was his love of children.[1] Friedrich Engels, who devoted much careful attention in later life to primitive Christianity and the New Testament canon, reached this feeble conclusion with regard to the person of Jesus Christ: 'Even the historical existence of a Jesus Christ can be regarded as open to question.'[2] Lenin, who contested with all his might the historicity of Jesus, praised the 'well-known German scholar' Arthur Drews and his book *The Christ Myth (Die Christusmythe*, 1909) because in it he refuted religious prejudices and legends, and proved that Christ had never existed.[3] Although Lenin went on to criticise Drews violently because he was advocating a revised, tidied-up and cunningly devised religion, in order to replace the old discredited religious prejudices by brand-new but still more obnoxious and objectionable ones, yet he affirmed an alliance with the progressive section of the bourgeoisie: 'for in the conflict with the dominant religious obscurantists some sort of "alliance" with Drews is for us a duty.'[4]

This statement of Lenin that Christ had never existed marks the end of the path begun by Feuerbach. When Feuerbach declared Jesus Christ to be the product of human need, he did not go so far as to dispute the historicity of Jesus. That task was attempted by the Frenchman Ernest Renan (1823-1892) and the German Arthur Drews (1865-1935) but it did not meet with any real success either in the historical or the theological field. Their life-long concern was much rather with atheism and free thinking. But it is remarkable that Drews' theory, which declared Jesus Christ to be a myth, did not entirely dominate materialistic atheism, although the more radical champions of atheism of course persisted in the denial of the historicity of Jesus. Since Feuerbach, Renan and Drews the expressions 'legendary Jesus' and 'mythical Christ'

[1] Lessner, 'Erinnerungen eines Arbeiters an Karl Marx', *Die Neue Zeit*, XI 1, p. 751.
[2] Marx-Engels, *On Religion*, p. 194.   [3] Lenin, *Religion*, p. 38.
[4] *Op. cit.*, p. 39.

are common in materialistic atheism without however becoming part of its general body of opinion.

The Account of Jesus Christ in the Historical Works of Mishulin and Mashkin

The two historical works of A. W. Mishulin, *History of Antiquity* (*Geschichte des Altertums*) and N. A. Mashkin, *History of Rome* (*Römische Geschichte*) are of particular significance. The attitude of materialistic atheism to Jesus Christ and Christianity is clearly indicated in Mishulin's book. Mishulin mentions Jesus Christ in connection with the increase of misery and oppression in the Roman Empire. Wandering preachers and prophets appeared all over the place to prepare the way for the Messiah. 'It was then that the myth of Jesus Christ, the God-man arose among the people, teaching that suffering must be endured patiently, because the sufferers and the oppressed would receive their reward in a future life. Sinners on the other hand were condemned to everlasting torment. This myth grew up under powerful oriental influence. It was at first circulated orally and only written down much later. In no historical documents of that time is there any word about the life of Jesus Christ.'[1] This quotation from Mishulin's *History of Antiquity* is a modification of a statement made in an earlier edition that science had proved that Jesus Christ had never existed. The more moderate version was produced as the result of protests.

In contrast with Mishulin the statements of Mashkin on the life, sufferings and death and resurrection of Jesus Christ appear more objective. Jesus Christ is referred to as the founder of the new religion: 'According to the new doctrine, in fulfilment of the Jewish Law and the ancient prophecies, a son was born in a miraculous way to the Virgin Mary in a town in Judea. When he grew to manhood he received baptism from the Jewish preacher John, called the Baptist, and devoted his life to the preaching of the true faith. He taught the people and performed miracles. By his acts he fulfilled the Law and the Prophets. But the Jewish priests and scribes hated him. Shortly before the feast of the

---

[1] Mishulin, *Geschichte des Altertums*, p. 203.

Passover he was betrayed by his disciple Judas, condemned by the Sanhedrin at Jerusalem and after being sentenced by the Roman procurator Pontius Pilate was crucified. On the third day Jesus rose from the dead, appeared to his disciples and then ascended into heaven. According to the teaching of the Evangelists, Jesus was the true Messiah, the Christ (i.e. the anointed). His death and resurrection mean the deliverance of men from original sin.'[1]

Accounts of Jesus Christ from History Textbooks of the East German Republic

The *Textbook for History Teaching in the Fifth School Year* (*Lehrbuch für den Geschichtsunterricht im 5. Schuljahr*, 1951) gives the following account of Jesus of Nazareth: 'In the Gospels it is related that Jesus was born during the reign of the Roman Emperor Caesar Augustus. It had been announced by an angel beforehand to his mother that she would bring the Son of God into the world. It is related further that when he grew to manhood he travelled from place to place preaching to the people, particularly to the poor. To the rich he said: "If you would be perfect, go and sell what you have and give it to the poor. . . . It is easier for a camel to go through the eye of a needle than for a rich man to enter the Kingdom of God." Christianity also teaches however that men should submit to and even endure injustice without resisting. It says in the Bible: "If someone strikes you on the right cheek, offer him the other. . . . Love your enemies, bless them that curse you, and do good to them that hate you." The Gospels tell of many miracles that Jesus is said to have performed. He is said to have restored dead people to life, to have walked on the water, and to have fed 5,000 people with five loaves and two fishes. He gathered a great number of followers round him. Twelve of his pupils, who are described as disciples, travelled with him from place to place.

'The Gospels give this account of the death of Jesus: "Jesus had come to Jerusalem and was preaching in the temple. Then the priests of the temple decided to capture Jesus by guile and have him killed. One of the twelve disciples, Judas Iscariot,

[1] Mashkin, *Römische Geschichte*, p. 551.

betrayed Jesus for thirty silver coins. Jesus was arrested and tried before the High Priest. Asked if he was Christ the Son of God, Jesus said he was. Then he was condemned to death.

'As Palestine was a Roman colony no death sentence could be carried out without the consent of the Roman governor. The Bible relates that consequently Jesus was brought before the governor, Pontius Pilate, who confirmed the death sentence. On the Friday before Easter Jesus was crucified. The Bible relates further that Jesus was laid in the tomb, but that he rose from the dead.'[1]

This extract on the life, sufferings, death and resurrection of Jesus Christ was considerably shortened in the 1952 edition,[2] but in tendency (non-committal reporting) both editions were alike. The 1953 edition cut out the account of the life and death of Jesus altogether, and only described Christianity.[3] In the 1957 edition of the *Textbook* this separate account of Christianity is also left out.

In the textbook for the teaching of History in the sixth school year called *Peasants, Townspeople and Feudal Lords (Bauern, Bürger und Feudalherren)* only the Church and monasteries in the tenth and eleventh centuries are mentioned. The only reference to Christ and Christianity is: 'When the Germanic tribes still believed in gods, the Christian faith arose in the far south in the countries around the Mediterranean. Its followers, the "Christians" did not worship many gods like the ancient Germans; they believed in one God only. The Christians became a community because of their common faith. This community was called the church.'[4]

The various editions of the textbook for the teaching of History

---

[1] *Lehrbuch für den Geschichtsunterricht, 5. Schuljahr*, Part 4, Berlin/Leipzig 1951, p. 52f; *ibid.*, Berlin/Leipzig 1951, p. 252f.

[2] *Lehrbuch für den Geschichtsunterricht, 5. Schuljahr*, Berlin 1952, p. 232.

[3] *Ibid.*, Berlin 1953, p. 177f, on Christianity: the idea of deliverance; the Christian communities; the recognition of Christianity; Constantinople the capital.

[4] Herbert Muhlstadt, *Lehrbuch für den Geschichtsunterricht, 6. Schuljahr (Bauern, Bürger und Feudalherren)*, Berlin 1957, p. 24; The corresponding textbook for the 5th school year, *Aus vergangener Zeit*, Berlin 1957, cut down the material considerably, so that only one page was left about the gods of the germanic tribes, and nothing at all about Christianity.

in the fifth and sixth school years thus show how from time to time the account given of Jesus Christ and Christianity was changed and systematically abridged. The first and most detailed account, that of 1951, is obviously put together hurriedly, and so is superficial and in parts confused. It gives the impartial reader no clear picture of Jesus, but deliberately creates a hostile prejudice against him. It is, therefore, preferable that the editions subsequent to 1953 have left out the distorted account altogether and have confined themselves to incidental references to Christianity. In contrast to the textbook for the fifth school year, the textbook for History teaching in the ninth school year omits any account of Jesus Christ altogether and confines itself to a totally false description of the origin of the New Testament writings.[1]

Other Statements of Materialistic Atheism about Jesus Christ

The account of Jesus Christ and Christianity in the textbooks for History teaching, and in Mishulin and Mashkin, represent some of the most important modern statements by materialistic atheism in the German language. Hatred or deliberate distortion is least apparent in Mashkin; he strives for the greatest objectivity, so that his few lines offer a more accurate picture of Jesus than the longer statements in the *Textbook*. The well-known encyclopaedia, *Lexikon A-Z* maintains a certain reserve. Under the heading 'Jesus' it says: 'A carpenter's son, who was born in Bethlehem and grew up in Nazareth. His passionate struggle for uncompromising fulfilment of the ethical commandments of the Jewish religion aroused the hostility of the official representatives of Jewish orthodoxy, who with the help of the Roman occupying power, had him executed about AD 28.'[2] Nevertheless this Lexicon cannot resist under the heading 'Christianity' calling in question the historicity of Jesus, with the observation that Jesus of Nazareth is not historically recognized[3] and reliable information about him apart from the Bible is lacking.[4]

[1] *Lehrbuch für den Geschichtsunterricht*, 9. *Schuljahr*, Part 4, Berlin 1952, p. 74f; *ibid.*, Berlin 1953, p. 275ff; *ibid.*, Berlin 1954 and 1955.
[2] *Lexikon A-Z*, Leipzig 1953, p. 472; *ibid*, 1956, vol. 1, p. 853.
[3] *Op. cit.*, p. 166. The 1956 edition omits this.
[4] *Op. cit.*, p. 472. The 1956 edition omits this.

In comparison with the accounts of Jesus Christ and Christianity already mentioned the specifically atheistic statements of men like A. P. Gagarin are much less important. At the very beginning of his pamphlet on *The Origin and Class Character of Christianity* (*Die Entstehung und Klassencharakter des Christentums*), 1955, he says: 'The Fathers of the Church created on the basis of the Gospel myth the legend that Christianity arose through the divine appearance of Christ on earth. According to this legend the founder of Christianity was the Son of God, Jesus Christ, who was miraculously born of the Virgin Mary by immaculate conception through the Holy Spirit. He raised the dead, healed the sick, preached the foundation of the new religion, then was crucified in Jerusalem, but rose again by a miracle and ascended into heaven.'[1] By way of comment on this remarkable theory of Gagarin it is enough to say: Neither logically nor above all historically is there any evidence that Christianity and the Fathers of the Church were first present, and that the latter invented the legend of Jesus Christ. Here as so often there is an inadmissible perversion of historically demonstrable events, a perversion which, in view of all that we know about Christ, Christendom and the founding of the Church (Pentecost), is unconvincing and is obviously an unhistorical invention.

M. Karpov, a philosophy student, speculating on 'How the modern system of reckoning dates arose' writes that in the sixth century the Roman monk Dionysius suggested dating the reckoning of time from a fictitious incident, the birth of Christ. In order to establish the belief in the existence of Christ Dionysius attempted to confirm the choice of this year by astronomical calculation. According to the church legend the first Easter (the resurrection of Christ) fell on March 25th. This was formerly the date of the beginning of the celebration of the mysteries in honour of Adonis, a Phoenician god. The cult of Adonis was widespread in Greece and Rome. 'With a little adjustment it was later transformed into a Christ-cult.' Thus a purely arbitrary date became the basis of the Christian reckoning of time.[2]

---

[1] Gagarin, *Die Entstehung*, p. 3.
[2] Karpov, 'Wie die heutige Zeitrechnung zustande kam', *SUP*, 1955/100/2171.

Materialistic atheism has also commented on the discovery of the Dead Sea Scrolls at Qumran. This is regarded as evidence against the historicity of Jesus. A. P. Kashdan, a student of History, reports: The author of the Habakkuk commentary mentions a 'teacher of righteousness', the Messiah, who is identified by some investigators with Jesus Christ of the Gospels. These scholars seem to be trying to prove with the help of the Qumran documents that Jesus Christ really existed and was the founder of the Christian religion. 'It is well known that theologians and church historians have been trying in vain for a century to find documents to prove that Jesus Christ, the chief figure in the Gospels was an actual historical person. Scientific criticism has shown that the Gospels are a later literary production, full of contradictions, errors and improbable stories, and are therefore incredible. Moreover, the Greek, Roman and Jewish writers, describing the Palestine of the first century, do not mention Christ, although they give details of the Essenes[1] among others. Even by such authors as Josephus Flavius and his opponent Justus of Tiberias Christ is not mentioned, although these authors were living in Palestine at the time and must have heard of Christ and the Christians, if there had been any Christians at the beginning of the first century. Today it is definitely and fully proved that these manuscripts date from the second and first centuries before our era, i.e. before the alleged "birth of Christ". Earlier some scholars, (the French scholar Renan and the Soviet scientist R. J. Wipper) had drawn attention to the similarity between the Essenes and the early Christian communities. The Qumran documents support this hypothesis. They show particularly that the figure of the messenger of God, the teacher of righteousness, had been known among the Essenes long before the time when the Gospels say the legendary Christ was born. Consequently the outlines of the figure of Christ had been already present in religious legend, before the rise of Christianity. The teaching of the Essenes, about which we now know much more than before the discovery of the Dead Sea Scrolls, was one of those intellectual currents that prepared the rise of Christianity.'[2]

[1] Essenes—a late Jewish sect from the second century B.C. to the first century A.D. Their chief seat was possibly the monastery at Qumran.
[2] Kashdan, 'Handschriften erzählen', *SUP*, 1957/55.

The most radical denial of the historicity of Jesus occurs however in the work of German authors: *Notes for Private Study for Middle School Teachers in the Faculty of History* (*Lehrbriefe für das Fernstudium der Mittelstufenlehrer, Fach Geschichte*), which was admittedly printed for private circulation only. In it special emphasis is laid on the 'culture of the period of the Roman emperors', i.e. architecture, literature, law and the spread of oriental cults. On Christianity it says: 'For the creation of the figure of its founder Christianity made use of the idea of the Messiah, which was widespread in the different religions of the East, particularly in Judaism.' Christianity became victorious over the other religions because it appealed to the interests of both the oppressed and the slave owners. It stressed particularly sharply Christ's sympathy for the 'weary and heavy laden', whose suffering and sins he took upon himself. 'Here the question of the historicity of Jesus has to be decided. Not until the relatively late period did the transformation of Christ into a historical person begin. In Marcion[1] (about AD 150) Jesus was still represented as coming down from heaven and appearing at Capernaum.'[2]

These statements of materialistic atheism about Jesus Christ will be enough. What is surprising is the number of these statements and the variety of viewpoint. Nowhere is there a disrespectful word about Christ, instead there is even sometimes a certain respect for the figure of the Son of Man. There is certainly some perplexity about the person Jesus, which leads to some remarkable conclusions. This confusion is more obvious in the observation about the Qumran MSS.: 'the outlines of the figure of Christ' were formed before the rise of Christianity. On the other hand it is said that Christianity, or the Fathers of the Church created the figure of Christ.

Neither of these two versions does justice to the claims of historical research on the sources. How can documents from pre-Christian centuries furnish proof of the unhistoricity of a person who lived centuries later? The reference to Marcion and his theology is just as questionable. Because of his distance from the

---

[1] Marcion—from Pontus in Asia Minor, founder of an important sect.
[2] *Lehrbriefe für das Fernstudium der Mittelstufenlehrer, Fach Geschichte,* Book 5, Berlin 1955, p. 403.

lifetime of Jesus he is of little importance compared with the eye-witness reports and the critical study of the Gospels and the authors of the apostolic letters.

There are still questions not adequately answered by those who deny the historicity of Jesus: Who, singly or collectively, is the inventor of the figure of Jesus witnessed to in the four Gospels supposed to have been? Which (obviously nameless) person, which actual community, or as materialistic atheism puts it, which slaves and oppressed people are supposed to have produced the myth of Jesus Christ, in view of the fact that the Gospels produced to the world Jesus of Nazareth as the Christ of God so vividly, in such detail and independently, and on the whole with such unanimity and yet such varied aspects? Where and when is this supposed to have happened? The internal evidence of the Gospels is so overwhelming and unimaginable, especially since the numerous differences and contradictions have not been smoothed over but left there, that to deny the historicity of Jesus necessitates more and more new theories, even including the transferring of the rise of Christianity from the first to the second century. To explain the Gospels and Christianity as the work of charlatans was abandoned even by Engels and other materialistic atheists in contrast to the French materialists of the eighteenth century.[1] Since all the biblical criticism and the denial of the historicity of Jesus in the nineteenth century no intelligent reasons for the rise of Christianity apart from Jesus Christ have been produced. The witness of the New Testament to Christ rests on the ground of four believable and very conscientious witnesses to Jesus of Nazareth, who knew himself to be the Son of God, and whom the Christian communities from the beginning until today have so confessed and still confess. Men can refuse the claim of Jesus and the revealing acts of God on their own responsibility but it is not possible for them to deny the life of Jesus as a man among men. The testimony of the evangelists and apostles is too good and too convincing for that. Whoever contests the historicity of Jesus is faced with the serious task of explaining how else Christianity arose.

[1] Marx-Engels, *On Religion*, p. 194.

Materialistic Atheism on the Rise of Christianity

Looking at the statements of materialistic atheism about Jesus Christ, one is struck by the fact that a clear distinction is often made between the figure of Christ and Christianity. Only Mashkin calls Jesus definitely 'the founder of the new religion'.[1] In general materialistic atheism avoids attributing Christianity to the person and activity of Jesus Christ. Perhaps that is most bluntly indicated in Gagarin's contention that the 'Fathers of the Church' were the inventors of the legend of Jesus Christ, so that accordingly Christ was not the founder of Christianity, but Christianity was the inventor of Jesus Christ.[2] This view postulates and constructs a Christianity without Christ, simply as a sociological phenomenon. That is what most of the hypotheses of materialistic atheism on the rise of Christianity lead to.

When materialistic atheism sets Christianity in its historical perspective, it is not only in order to show the interrelation of Christianity with the world around it, but mainly in order to give a logical historical explanation of its origin. That is at once apparent in the literary treatment of Christianity. In the larger historical works of materialistic atheism Christianity is never treated as an independent or original entity, but always as the product of particular epochs and circumstances. Thus the *Textbook for History Teaching in the Fifth School Year* connects Christianity with the decline and collapse of the Roman slave state, particularly with the economic decline of the Roman Empire.[3] The *Textbook for History Teaching in the Ninth School Year*, on the other hand, describes Christianity as the product of oriental cults.[4] Mishulin mentions Christianity only in connection with Diocletian (284-305)[5] whereas Mashkin describes primitive Christianity in relation to Roman culture and the spread of oriental cults in the first and second centuries.[6]

In all these cases the intention is to create the impression that

[1] Mashkin, *Römische Geschichte*, p. 551.
[2] Gagarin, *Die Entstehung*, p. 3.
[3] *Lehrbuch für den Geschichtsunterricht*, 5. *Schuljahr*, Part 4, Berlin/Leipzig 1951, p. 49ff.
[4] *Ibid.*, 9. *Schuljahr*, Part 4, Berlin 1952, p. 74ff.
[5] Mishulin, *Geschichte des Altertums*, p. 201ff.
[6] Mashkin, *Römische Geschichte*, p. 543ff.

Christianity is the product of some natural processes and circumstances, the result of economic or political decay, the effect of Roman culture, or the influence of oriental cults. The obvious and most natural idea that Christianity goes back to the life and work of Jesus Christ is in general carefully avoided and deliberately by-passed. A typical example is *Universe, Earth and Man,* that devotes fifty lines of print to the explanation of the rise of Christianity without ever mentioning the name of Jesus Christ.[1]

The attempt of materialistic atheism to explain Christianity mainly as a sociological phenomenon and as far as possible to avoid attributing it to the work of Jesus Christ, and to account for it by contemporary historical conditions, is not an original idea: it stands on the shoulders of its middle-class predecessors in the eighteenth and nineteenth centuries, particularly Strauss, Feuerbach and Bruno Bauer. Anyone who refuses to recognize Jesus Christ as a historic figure and denies that he was the founder of Christianity, must obviously hunt out all possible and impossible factors in order to be able to explain the origin of Christianity without Christ. In this undertaking materialistic atheism greedily snatched up almost all the ideas that have been put forward up till the end of the nineteenth century about the history of Christianity. Friedrich Engels particularly, from the same viewpoint, turned his attention again in later life to the origin of Christianity, and published three separate essays on it.[2]

Engels described the conditions favourable to the rise of Christianity as mainly economic and social, i.e. misery, want, exploitation, 'injustice and despair, apathy and demoralization'. 'What popular philosophy did in Greece and Rome, Roman domination and the replacement of free proud men by desperate yes-men and selfish scoundrels did in the colonies. That was the material and moral situation. The present was intolerable, the future was if possible even more menacing. . . . But in every class there must have been people who were looking for spiritual deliverance, an inner consolation as a substitute for material relief. There was no comfort to be found in the Stoa or in the

---

[1] *Weltall, Erde und Mensch,* Berlin 1954, p. 299f; *ibid.,* 1956, p. 364; *ibid.* 1959, p. 339.
[2] See p. 73, n. 1.

school of Epicurus: . . . it could only come in a religious form. . . .
Most of those who were longing for such consolation must have
been amongst the slaves. And then into this general economic,
political, intellectual and moral disintegration came Christianity.
It was a complete contrast to all religions before then.'[1]

The shocking conditions in the Roman Empire at the end of the
first century BC form an essential element in the materialistic-
atheistic theory about the origin of Christianity. The idea of social
misery as the decisive factor in the rise and spread of Christianity
still plays an important part in modern atheistic literature. The
Textbook for History Teaching in its account of Christianity makes
a great point of the intolerable living conditions of the masses in
the Roman Empire, in order to stress the longing for deliverance
from so much misery and to account for the wide and swift spread
of Christianity.[2] *Universe, Earth and Man* also draws attention to
misery, want and oppression to explain why the 'weary and heavy
laden' lent a willing ear to the belief in deliverance.[3] Gagarin goes
a step further and says: 'The legends and fairy-tales of the Gospels
about Jesus would never have grown up amongst the slaves and
subject peoples, and would never have drawn whole nations under
their spell, if men had not been thirsting for fairy-tales, and if
living conditions had not existed which gave rise to them.' 'This
fairy-tale arose because reality was so desolate and joyless. Hope-
less slavery without any ray of light—that was the cause of the rise
of the Christian religion and also the Christ legend.'[4]

However useful the description of social misery in the Roman
Empire at the time of the birth of Christ may be in accounting for
the rapid spread of Christianity, it provides nothing to explain
the origin of Christianity, i.e. the life and work of Jesus himself.
For it is utterly impossible to explain the incarnation of Jesus by
any condition of the material world, by particular social-economic
circumstances: it depends solely on the decision of God (Gal.
4.4; II Cor. 5.19). To explain the origin of Christianity by social

[1] Marx-Engels, *On Religion*, p. 201.
[2] *Lehrbuch für den Geschichtsunterricht, 5. Schuljahr*, Part 4, Berlin/Leipzig,
1951, p. 51.
[3] *Weltall, Erde und Mensch*, 1954, p. 301.
[4] Gagarin, *Die Entstehung*, p. 20.

conditions is nothing more than to give a historical and material setting to the idea already developed by Marx: 'Religious misery is at once the expression of material misery and a protest against it. Religion is the sign of the oppressed creature, the heart of a heartless world, the soul of soulless conditions.'[1] However much truth there may be in this idea of Marx, the longing for deliverance is not sufficient to account for the appearance of an actual deliverer. The postulate does not guarantee the reality.

Engels, following Bruno Bauer, also said the final word about the original character of Christianity, as far as materialistic atheism is concerned. Engels maintained that Christianity was a popular revolutionary movement: 'Christianity like every other revolutionary movement was the creation of the masses.' 'Christianity was originally a movement of the oppressed.' 'Both great movements, primitive Christianity and Socialism, were not produced by leaders and prophets, although there were prophets enough in both; they were mass movements.'[2] Engels even maintains that after the fall of the Western Roman Empire a form of Socialism—as far as was then possible—came to power, i.e. Christianity.

The idea that Christianity was originally a popular revolutionary movement is readily adopted, repeated and elaborated by modern representatives of materialistic atheism, by Gagarin for example, who writes: 'Christianity arose as a protest of the slaves and subject peoples against the yoke of slavery.'[3] Mishulin offers a similar opinion: 'Engels points out that Christianity was originally a movement of the oppressed, and arose as a religion of slaves, freed men, the poor and legally underprivileged, and the peoples conquered and subjugated by Rome.'[4]

Finally Mashkin writes, quoting Engels: 'Primitive Christianity first appeared as a religion of slaves and freed men, the poor and legally underprivileged, the scattered peoples subjugated by Rome.'[5]

On the philosophical sources of Christianity Engels says, again

[1] Marx-Engels, *On Religion*, p. 42.   [2] *Op. cit.*, pp. 206, 313, 327.
[3] Gagarin, *Die Entstehung*, p. 8.
[4] Mishulin, *Geschichte des Altertums*, p. 203.
[5] Mashkin, *Römische Geschichte*, p. 553.

following Bruno Bauer, who saw the roots of Christianity in Stoicism and Judaism: 'Philo[1] was the real father of Christianity, and Seneca[2] was its uncle.'[3] Christianity is a hybrid phenomenon which became a doctrine through the addition of the teaching of the Alexandrian Jew Philo and later through strong Stoic infiltration.[4] This assertion of a twofold origin of Christianity, one Jewish and one Greek, is however not retained by Engels. In other places he stresses the predominant influence of Judaism: 'Of course Christianity only represents a sect of Judaism.'[5] Christianity developed from the Jewish religious reforms of AD 69.[6] The Jewish religion contributed to Christianity under strong Alexandrian influence. After that everything else was western Greco-Roman accretion.[7]

What Engels said about the philosophical sources of Christianity, following Bruno Bauer, is regarded by modern materialistic atheism as proven, and is often accepted without any critical comment. The *Textbook for History Teaching* mentions the Mithras cult as a precursor of Christianity.[8] Another edition of the same book describes in this connection the cults of Cybele, Isis, Mithras, and also Judaism and Philo.[9] Before his account of Christianity Mashkin describes cults from Asia Minor, Syria, Egypt and Persia and gives details of Judaism and Philo.[10] *Universe, Earth and Man* summarizes a number of oriental 'deliverance cults'.[11] Gagarin, going much further than Engels, writes: 'Besides its main ideological sources, Platonism and Stoicism, Christianity absorbed numerous religious myths and rites from Greek-oriental cults. Thus the myth and cult of the divine suffering, dying and rising saviour became part of Christian doctrine. Many legends and rites belonging to the Egyptian Osiris,

---

[1] Philo of Alexandria: b. between 30 and 20 BC, Hellenistic Jewish philosopher.

[2] Seneca: Roman author and philosopher, died AD 65.

[3] Marx-Engels, *On Religion*, pp. 195 and 206.

[4] *Op. cit.*, p. 206.   [5] *Op. cit.*, p. 207.   [6] *Op. cit.*, p. 330.

[7] *Op. cit.*, p. 342f.

[8] *Lehrbuch für den Geschichtsunterricht, 5. Schuljahr*, Part 4, Berlin/Leipzig 1951, p. 51.

[9] *Ibid., 9. Schuljahr*, Part 4, Berlin 1952, p. 74.

[10] Mashkin, *Römische Geschichte*, pp. 545-8.

[11] *Weltall, Erde und Mensch*, 1954, p. 300.

the Phrygian Attis, the Greek Dionysus and others were taken over into Christian doctrine.'[1]

The attempts of modern materialistic atheism to explain Christianity as a syncretic product are basically only variations on Engels' view: 'The new world religion, Christianity, had already arisen almost unnoticed from a mixture of generalized oriental theology, particularly the Jewish and popular Greek philosophy, especially Stoicism.'[2]

Engels' theory about the geographical location of the rise of Christianity fits in with what he has written about its circumstances, original character and philosophic sources, and which modern materialistic atheism has put forward as the attitude of science. On one hand Engels sees the rise of Christianity in Palestine: 'Christianity arose in a completely unknown way in Palestine at a time when new sects, new religions, new prophets were cropping up by the hundred.'[3] On the other hand he opposed flatly the opinion that Palestine was the location of the rise of Christianity: 'The legend of Christianity as arising ready-made from Judaism, conquering the world from Palestine with a mostly rigid dogma and ethic, has become untenable since Bruno Bauer.' Bauer has provided evidence to prove 'that Christianity was not imported into and forced upon the Greco-Roman world from Judea, but at least in its form as a world religion was the product of that world itself.'[4] Similarly Engels says in another place: 'Not Galilee and Jerusalem, but Alexandria and Rome are, according to Bauer, the birthplace of the new religion.'[5] Finally Engels expresses the opinion that Christianity had its main location in Asia Minor in the year 68.[6]

These contentions of materialistic atheism about the origin of Christianity are out of date in almost every particular and can no longer be sustained in face of the present state of scientific knowledge. They are based on an aversion to Christianity and are intended to refute and defeat it. Engels' dependence on Bruno Bauer has been disastrous and has obscured his vision of the real

[1] Gagarin, *Die Entstehung*, p. 15.
[2] Engels, *Ludwig Feuerbach*, p. 66.
[3] Marx-Engels, *On Religion*, p. 206.   [4] *Op. cit.*, p. 321.   [5] *Ibid.*
[6] *Op. cit.*, p. 339.

character of Christianity. In 1882 Engels confesses that Bruno Bauer has been more valuable and done more to illuminate the historical origin of Christianity than the official theologians.[1] Engels was obviously attracted by Bauer's 'remorseless criticism of the Gospels and the apostolic Epistles' but in the end found himself unable to support any longer Bauer's nihilistic radicalism: Bauer had far overshot the mark; he had put the rise of Christianity half a century later than was admissible and had taken wide liberties in his account of history. As a result, in Bauer's account every bit of historical background for the New Testament stories about Jesus and his disciples had vanished: he dissolved them into legends. Engels' enthusiasm for Bauer eventually cooled considerably, because the well-founded objections of experts against Bauer's exaggerated arguments had not been without effect on him. Nevertheless Engels clung to Bauer's distorted theories and was only partially persuaded of a better one.

Summing up, the following comments can be made on the explanation of the origin of Christianity put forward by materialistic atheism.

The original character of Christianity was a matter of faith, not of economics or social system. It cannot be traced back to slaves, to the masses, as Engels, Kautsky and Mehring tried to show, but only to the figure of Jesus Christ. Christianity can be looked at sociologically but cannot be explained sociologically.

The objectivity, originality and sovereignty of Jesus are simply overlooked in the theories of materialistic atheism. Anyone with a spark of historical sense left must admit that Jesus of Nazareth lived as a man in Palestine and claimed to be the Son of God.

The preaching of Jesus and his apostles did not, of course, take place in a vacuum, but took over and refashioned a good deal of existing material, mainly Israelite and Jewish, but also some Greek and oriental material. But just as the figure of Jesus Christ cannot be explained by his environment, so his message cannot be derived either from the circumstance of the time nor from historical-philosophic sources. But to remove the location of the rise of

[1] *Op. cit.*, p. 194.

Christianity from Palestine to Rome is to do violence to all the sources.

In its historical development Christianity unfortunately suffered under the process of contamination and of a tendency to religious-philosophic rigidity, but over and over again it was able to draw strength from the Gospel, as Jesus and the apostles had preached it, to renew itself and to shed all the accretions extraneous to the Gospel.

Materialistic Atheism on the Nature and Value of Christianity

As we have seen, materialistic atheism leaves a certain room for variation in its attitude to Christ and to the origin of Christianity. The same is true of its fundamental view of the nature and value of Christianity. This depends on its own basic outlook, which provides the criterion by which the nature and value of Christianity is judged. In recent years in materialistic atheism generally the view has persisted that primitive Christianity is in certain aspects positively approved as a movement amongst slaves and freed-men. Where Christianity is supposed to have originally appeared as a protest of the poorest against social misery, materialistic atheism shows increasing sympathy with the slaves and the oppressed within the Christian movement.

This positive appraisal of primitive Christianity is seen most convincingly in *Universe, Earth and Man*: 'The doctrine of the equality of all men, the demand for common ownership that was a characteristic feature of the oldest Christian communities, exactly matched the needs and demands of the oppressed and exploited section of the people. These demands found an echo in the doctrine of loving one's neighbour and the brotherhood of men, whether rich or poor, free or slaves. The social content of this doctrine was a powerful factor in the eager acceptance of this religion by the masses.'[1] The *Textbook for History Teaching in the Fifth School Year*, 1951 edition, commends in primitive Christianity the common meals, the mutual support, the recognition of the common humanity without regard to nationality, cultural or social position, the care for a dignified burial even of slaves, who were

[1] *Weltall, Erde und Mensch*, 1954, p. 300.

usually hurriedly buried in common burial grounds. On account of these arrangements Christianity had a distinct advantage over other deliverance religions and many of the poor in the towns felt attracted by it.[1] Mishulin mentions as commendable features of primitive Christianity the common meals, the mutual help to find work, and the common organization of the communities in the towns, that attracted the poorer section of the population.[2]

In his detailed account of Christianity Mashkin mentions very many commendable features of primitive Christianity. On the basis of the *Didache* (*The Teaching of the Twelve Apostles*) and the 'Acts' he develops the following description of the life of the early Christian communities: 'It was characterized by the eschatological mood of the early Christians and their confidence in the speedy return of Christ, by which men should not be taken by surprise, but for which they should rather be normally prepared. Hence the doctrine of the necessity for moral purification, with which also the idea of love and brotherhood was associated. Acts shows that the early Christian communities were familiar with common ownership of goods. Charity was developed to an extraordinary degree. The congregations were in contact with each other. Some of their members carried on a correspondence and sent delegates to each other. Travelling apostles and preachers, going from place to place, maintained contact between members of different Christian congregations.'[3] While materialistic atheism generally accepts Engel's view that the early Christians drew their adherents from the people belonging to the lowest strata of society,[4] Mashkin thinks that the composition of the Christian congregations was very mixed from the beginning. But he is also impressed by the humanistic features, as expressed in Col. 3.11, and quoted by Mashkin in German and Greek: 'There is neither Greek nor Jew, circumcision nor uncircumcision, Barbarian, Scythian, bond nor free, but Christ is all in all.' Mashkin draws from this the conclusion: 'Thus Christianity was against nationalistic religious

[1] *Lehrbuch für den Geschichtsunterricht*, 5. *Schuljahr*, Part 4, Berlin/Leipzig 1951, p. 51f.
[2] Mishulin, *Geschichte des Altertums*, p. 203.
[3] Mashkin, *Römische Geschichte*, p. 551.
[4] Marx-Engels, *On Religion*, p. 201.

exclusiveness. Former heathen from many different ethnic groups began very early to play an important part in Christianity. The idea of equality, which we meet amongst the Stoics and the Roman jurists, was realized more logically amongst the Christians than in other religions. Christianity proclaimed that all men were brothers, that slaves and free men were equal. It appealed particularly to the "weary and heavy laden", to whom it promised relief; it commended the poor as blessed and promised comfort to the mourners.'[1]

The Textbook for History Teaching in the Ninth School Year likewise expresses commendation of primitive Christianity also based, as in the case of Mashkin, on the Acts of the Apostles and the *Teaching of the Twelve Apostles*: 'The Christians of the first and second centuries believed in the speedy return of Christ. They wanted to be morally prepared for this. Hence arose the doctrine of the necessity for a radical purification with which the idea of love and brotherhood was associated. In the Acts there are allusions to common ownership of goods in the Christian communities. Charity was regarded as a Christian duty. Membership of the Christian communities was open to anyone who confessed the Christian doctrine, no matter to what race he belonged, or whether he were poor or rich, free or slave.'[2]

Although the authors of the works so far mentioned find comparatively numerous commendable features in primitive Christianity, Gagarin, as might be expected, is much more cautious in his commendation. Gagarin sees the 'progressive-democratic features of primitive Christianity' in the hope of the slaves and subject peoples for a change in the existing situation and for equality and brotherhood among men. Christianity was a dream of heaven on earth, of the millennial Kingdom of God, of freedom, equality and brotherhood of all men. 'The rumour current everywhere at that time that in the Christian communities equality between slaves and free men, between barbarians and Romans, was an accomplished reality, that there was within them mutual brotherly help between slaves and free Romans, Jews, Greeks and

---

[1] Mashkin, *Römische Geschichte*, p. 552.
[2] *Lehrbuch für den Geschichtsunterricht, 9. Schuljahr*, Part 4, Berlin 1952, p. 77.

prisoners of war (Barbarians) made early Christianity extra-
ordinarily popular.' But this belief in the realization of equality
between slaves and free men on earth, this progressive-democratic
feature of the primitive Christian movement of slaves, remained
unrealized, and what was originally a progressive-democratic
feature of the Christian movement among the slaves very soon
came under the ban of the politics and ideology of the slave-
owners, so that any real struggle for the equality of all men on
earth came to be regarded by the Church as sinful.[1]

Recognition of commendable features of primitive Christianity
by materialistic atheism has since been mostly suppressed or at
least greatly modified. The traces of common ownership of goods
in early Christianity are attributed to the cohesion of the persecuted rather than to genuine ideas of equality.[2] The cultural
significance of primitive Christianity is to some extent recognized,
in that it brought the barbarians into contact with Roman culture
and in this sense Christianity is admitted to have played a 'great
positive part'.[3] But these commendable features of primitive
Christianity are after all few in number and do not compensate for
the overall negative judgment on Christianity as a whole.

According to *Universe, Earth and Man*, Christian teaching
misleads men to a 'flight to other-worldliness' and diverts the
masses from the struggle for freedom.[4] This charge is levelled at
religion in general and at Christianity in particular. Still worse
than distraction from the struggle for freedom is, in the view of
materialistic atheism, that rich people joined the Christian
churches, who certainly made donations to the community, but
thereby caused the wealth of the church to increase.[5] The influx of
prosperous circles into the Christian churches[6] led to the creation
of the office of bishop (the episcopate, which is described generally
as the office of administration of wealth), a 'clerical bureaucracy'
leading to changes in doctrine and finally to reconciliation with
the state.

[1] Gagarin, *Die Entstehung*, p. 8.   [2] *Ibid.*
[3] Mishulin, *Geschichte des Altertums*, p. 204.
[4] *Weltall, Erde und Mensch*, 1954, p. 300.
[5] *Lehrbuch für den Geschichtsunterricht*, 9. *Schuljahr*, Part 4, Berlin 1952,
p. 77.
[6] Mishulin, *Geschichte des Altertums*, p. 203.

The persecution of the Christians is sometimes treated very seriously by atheistic writers.[1] Mashkin gives an objective and detailed account of this, though with a warning against exaggeration.[2] Gagarin, on the other hand, has a lot to say about the revolts of the slaves in the Roman Empire,[3] but does not mention the persecution of the Christians. *Universe, Earth and Man* mentions the refusal of Emperor worship by the Christians and their attack on the existing order, but then, only twice in all the editions, refers to the so-called persecutors of the Christians in order to belittle them and consign them to the realm of fairy tales.[4]

Thus materialistic atheism sees in the accession of wealthy people and the reconciliation with the state the real decline and specific corruption of the 'progressive-democratic movement of the slaves and the oppressed'. Gagarin describes the process of deterioration of primitive Christianity in a graphic and forthright way: The representatives of the slave-owning class acquired the leading position in the Christian churches for themselves. 'The prosperous "overseers" of the churches (bishops) gradually got the entire government of the Christian churches into their own hands. Above the bishops were the archbishops, and over them the metropolitans. At the top of the hierarchical ladder were the patriarchs.'[5]

The recognition of Christianity by Constantine the Great[6] is generally regarded as the end of the positive significance of early Christianity. 'Thus early Christianity as a democratic movement of the slaves was demolished from the inside by the clergy, and in time transformed into a mythical reactionary ideology and system of ethics advantageous to the exploiting classes—"opium" and "spiritual dope" for the masses.'[7]

From that point onwards materialistic atheism finds nothing

---

[1] *Lehrbuch für den Geschichtsunterricht, 5. Schuljahr;* also *9. Schuljahr;* also Mishulin, *Geschichte des Altertums.*
[2] Mashkin, *Römische Geschichte*, pp. 556-558.
[3] Gagarin, *Die Entstehung*, p. 7f.
[4] *Weltall, Erde und Mensch*, 1954, p. 300f.
[5] Gagarin, *Die Entstehung*, p. 10.
[6] In 313. It marked the end of persecution in the Roman Empire, equality of status, indeed preferential status, for Christianity, but also the rise of the state church.
[7] *Op. cit.*, p. 13.

good in the Christian Church. It turned to the Christian sects, the opposition, the Chiliasts and Montanists.[1] The original 'anti-plutocratic tendency' in the early Christian teaching,[2] as in the often-quoted saying of Jesus about the eye of a needle (Matt. 19.24; Mark 10.25; Luke 18.25),[3] and the social tendency of the Gospel of St Luke, had been transformed into an approximation to the slave-owning state and active support for the politics of the Emperor.[4]

According to materialistic atheism the development of Christianity from what was originally a religion of the exploited into a later religion of the exploiters, with a corresponding reversal of the commendation of early Christianity into condemnation of later Christianity, has recently found classic expression in the *Textbook of German History*: 'While Christianity was originally a religion of slaves and the poor . . . it later gradually developed . . . into the ally of the ruling class.'[5]

From this view of primitive Christianity and the history of the early Church it goes on to the scathing judgment: 'The Christian religion, which preaches humility and servile submission to the exploiters, hinders the workers from the class struggle and thus plays a reactionary role in modern social history.'[6] The Christian preaching of humility would help the oppression of the workers even today; for this reason Christianity is a reactionary ideology of the exploiters.[7] Mishulin reaches the same unfavourable judgment: 'The Church did not incite the masses to a class war. On the contrary it preached resignation and submission to the masters. We read in the Christian writings: "Servants be obedient to your masters, as to the symbol of God."'[8]

The overall judgment of materialistic atheism on Christianity is total condemnation. Marx considered Christianity not only untrue but also immoral.[9] Engels declared the Christian teaching

[1] *Op. cit.*, p. 12f.
[2] Mashkin, *Römische Geschichte*, p. 553: 'In primitive Christian teaching there was a quite definite anti-plutocratic tendency, the condemnation of wealth.'
[3] Mashkin (*op. cit.*, p. 553) even quotes the passages mentioned in Greek.
[4] Mashkin, *op. cit.*, p. 560.
[5] *Lehrbuch der deutschen Geschichte*, vol. I, Berlin 1960, p. 150.
[6] Gagarin, *Die Entstehung*, p. 7.   [7] *Op. cit.*, p. 21.
[8] Mishulin, *Geschichte des Altertums*, p. 204.
[9] *Marx-Engels Gesamtausgabe*, I 6, p. 369f.

to be 'nonsense preached by slaves and victims of oppression' and refers to Christianity as a 'nonsense religion.'[1] Accordingly he considers the writings of the satirist and scoffer Lucian of Samosata (*c.* 120-180) to be 'one of our best sources for the early Christians'.[2] The more modern atheistic writers reach a similar verdict on Christianity. Pavyolkin at the end of his description of the 'religious Christ-legend' adds, about the feeding of the multitude by the Sea of Galilee: 'Five thousand hungry people were fed with five loaves. That is impossible, a distortion of truth, a fantastic flight of the imagination, a fairy tale. We find the same imagination in every other religious notion.'[3] Gagarin thinks not only that the Gospel myths contain nothing original but also that 'The idea of "resist not evil" preached by Christianity supports the class interests of the slave owners, feudal lords and capitalists.'[4] Gagarin also points to the differing views of the 'mythical Christ', which represent the diverse and contrasting class interests of different periods.[5]

How are We to evaluate the Attitude of Materialistic Atheism to Jesus and to Christianity?

The larger number of different opinions expressed by materialistic atheism about Jesus and Christianity can be summarized in the following statements:

1. Materialistic Atheism alternates between Admission and Denial of the Historicity of Jesus

The statements made by materialistic atheism about Christ vary between two extremes. On one side is the recognition of Jesus of Nazareth as a historical person. In 1851 Engels agreed with Thomas Münzer that Jesus was an ordinary man. In 1882 on the other hand Engels said that hardly anything in the whole contents of the Gospels could be established historically, so that it could be said that even the historical existence of Jesus Christ was open to question.[6] The *Lexikon A-Z* does not deny the historicity of Jesus, but represents him as an uncompromising moral philosopher.

---

[1] Marx-Engels, *On Religion*, p. 194.   [2] *Op. cit.*, p. 315f.
[3] Pavyolkin, *Der religiöse Aberglaube*, p. 7.
[4] Gagarin, *Die Entstehung*, p. 5.   [5] Gagarin, *op. cit.*, p. 19f.
[6] Marx-Engels, *On Religion*, p. 194.

The other extreme of materialistic atheism is represented by all those statements which contest the historicity of Jesus and explain him as the creation of human imagination.

The beginning of this idea is to be found in Feuerbach's philosophy of religion. He explains the figure of Jesus as arising out of the religious needs of the human spirit. Thus Feuerbach reduces history to the product of the human mind. Most of the opinions of materialistic atheism about Christ rest on this conception of history.

Some statements of materialistic atheism do not so absolutely deny the historicity of Jesus, but attempt a compromise between historicity and the myth theory. Thus Bebel says that the existence of Christ is very dubious, and the *Lexikon A-Z* says that Christ is not clearly recognized historically.

The statements of materialistic atheism about the origin of Christianity are neither consistent nor clear. The very general verdicts of Engels and Mehring that Christianity as a world religion was a product of the Greco-Roman world[1] are no explanation. Bebel's statement that the Christian teaching was only the quintessence of the philosophical views of antiquity since Socrates and Plato[2] gives no adequate explanation, but is too general and inconsistent. There were attempts to explain the rise of Christianity on the basis of social, economic, political and cultural conditions, or by going back to Judaism, Greek Philosophy and a wide variety of oriental cults. But questions about the authors or inventors of the supposed myth of Jesus Christ only produce vague answers: that it arose amongst the common people (Mishulin), a vague reference to the Fathers of the Christian Church (Gargarin), or that Christianity used this or that for the creation of the figure of its founder (*Textbook*).

None of these statements can in any intelligent way account for the rise of Christianity or the creation of the New Testament.

Authors or inventors of myths would have produced one Gospel, not four. They would have avoided such concrete varying statements, so portentous for the first twelve disciples, and which

---

[1] *Op. cit.*, pp. 195 and 206.
[2] Bebel, *Ist die Religion für das Volk nötig ?*, Berlin 1958.

have been preserved in the four Gospels so faithfully and without any glossing over. They would have been able to dispense with the difficult epistles of Paul, Peter, and James, saturated with such very individual, material and personal reflections. It is evident, against the atheistic hypotheses, that neither Christianity nor the New Testament can be explained without Jesus Christ.

2. *Materialistic Atheism is not Concerned with Discovering the Truth about Jesus Christ but only with Refutation*

In his three works on primitive Christianity Friedrich Engels was guided by the following considerations: 'A religion which subdued the Roman Empire and dominated by far the greater part of the civilized world for 1,800 years, cannot be dismissed simply as rubbish put together by charlatans. It can only be dealt with when its origin and development are understood in relation to the historical conditions in which it arose and achieved power. The important thing is to solve the problem how it happened that the masses of the people in the Roman Empire came to prefer to all other religions this rubbish preached by slaves and victims of oppression, so that eventually the ambitious Constantine saw in the acceptance of this "nonsense religion" the best means of making himself the sole ruler of the Roman world' (Marx-Engels, *On Religion*, p. 194).

The important thing in this argument is that Engels is not concerned with understanding and explaining, but with 'how to deal with the Christian religion', i.e. with the possibility of refutation and defeat, with the rejection of everything Christian. This may account for the passionate way in which materialistic atheism concentrates on Christ and Christianity. But in so doing it loses the possibility of judging objectively and of doing justice to the person Jesus and the origin and development of Christianity.

This hostile attitude to Christianity gives rise to a lot of contradictions and absurdities. On the one hand there is supposed to be a similarity between heathen and Christian rites (Bebel) and on the other Christianity is said to offer a contrast to all other existing religions (Engels). On one hand it is not claimed that the Christian religion was the work of charlatans, and on the other

hand we meet expressions like the Christian 'nonsense religion'
and 'nonsense propaganda' (Engels). It does not look well for
Engels, for example, to commend an opponent of early Christianity
like Lucian of Samosata as an 'unbiassed witness' or to declare his
anti-Christian satire *On the Death of Perigrinus* to be 'one of our
best sources about the early Christians'. The Frenchman Ernest
Renan can scarcely be reckoned 'a scholar and expert' as Kashdan
calls him,[1] but only as a successful and imaginative writer of fiction.
As for Bruno Bauer, Engels himself later dissociated himself
vigorously from him, because his theories were historically untenable.

Materialistic atheism finds itself in an unpleasant dilemma over
the figure of Jesus Christ. Recently an attempt has been made to
resolve it by reviving the 'charlatan hypothesis'. In 1960 a 'study
group on philosophy' in the German Academy of Science in East
Berlin published a bilingual edition of the work *De Tribus
Impostoribus Anno MDIIC* (*On the Three Imposters, 1598*—Moses,
Jesus and Mohammed) as a source and text for the history of
philosophy. Although the publishers have admitted this anonymous work to be a forgery (it was not written in 1598 but much
later), the new impression was approved by the philosophy class
of the Academy. In the opinion of the publisher the attitude of
this work does not yet go as far as a completely developed atheism.
Asked the reason for a new edition of this particular 'charlatan
book', which has been shown to be a forgery,[2] the publisher
offered two reasons. Firstly the new edition of the 'charlatan
book' would help to build up a picture of the history of philosophy
that properly reflected the intellectual development in Germany.
In other words: the atheistic tradition is to be bolstered up and
assisted with the help of a forgery. The second reason for the new
edition was to follow Lenin's advice to republish and spread
amongst the people the disputations, the vivid and most able
publications of earlier atheists, in order to shake up the people
from their religious sleep.[3] The publisher of the 'charlatan book'
affirmed in 1960 the validity of this idea of Lenin and thinks it

[1] Kashdan, 'Handschriften erzählen', *SUP*, 1057/55.
[2] *De tribus impostoribus*, p. 36 (cf. p. 37, n. 4).
[3] Lenin, *Religion*, p. 37.

unnecessary to substantiate it further. Thus the staggering fact in
relation to this new publication is that an anonymous old forgery
(the contents of which are determined by completely out-of-date
speculation in the spirit of Spinoza) should be offered to students
of philosophy with intent to undermine beforehand the person and
work of Jesus of Nazareth and in order to charge Christianity and
the Church with fraud. It is clear that the last traces of intention
and effort at serious consideration of Christ and of Christians have
been distorted into a passionate hatred against the Gospel of God
in Christ.

3. A Distinction must be made between Christ and the Christian Religion, between the Gospel of Jesus and Christianity

As a result of the tribulations of the nineteenth and twentieth
centuries evangelical Christendom has found a new and lasting
understanding of the Christian faith, which must be made clear
beyond all doubt to materialistic atheism: a firm and clear distinction must be made between the figure of Jesus Christ, his words,
his deeds, his life, death and resurrection on the one hand and
what men, history and the 'Christian' states and nations have
made of it on the other. Apostasy, hypocrisy and disobedience on
the part of his people is no evidence against Jesus Christ, but is
the fault of Christians, for which they should be penitent. The
Gospel has become a true reality, not in Christianity, but only in
the Church in the sense of Article 7 of the Augsburg Confession:
'The Church is the congregation of believers in which the pure
Gospel is taught and the sacraments rightly administered.'
[Compare Article 19 of the 39 Articles.]

The Gospel and the Church are, like all the gifts of God, not
protected against misuse (cf. the story of the Fall, Gen. 3, and the
Temptation of Jesus, Matt. 4). Again and again the Gospel has
suffered corruption at the hands of men. The Church, in so far as
it is made up of men, has been disfigured, but in the mercy of God
has again been reformed. Some words of Jesus are easily misused
to support a religious ideology, but again and again they have been
commended to the world by his followers as signs and media
of God's gracious action. The New Testament Gospel is often

distorted into mere religion, but it turns out again and again to be the power of God (cf. Rom. 1.16-17). Against this process of illegitimate adaptation of the Gospel to the pattern of this world, forces have again and again operated to insist upon the independence of the Gospel and separation from the world. Believers have again and again resisted the confusion of the Gospel with all sorts of other forces and movements, finding their way back to the pure word of Jesus and delivering the Gospel from extraneous associations.

4. Atheistic Criticism of Christianity contains some Justified Reproaches, but also some that are Unfounded

Once the distinction between the Gospel and Christianity is made clear, the Christian faith can face confidently even those charges by materialistic atheism which are justified. Materialistic atheism shows little appreciation of the Gospel, but some slight understanding of primitive Christianity. Materialistic atheism sees an early decline of primitive Christianity caused by the fact that many rich people joined the Church and manipulated its teaching and way of life in their own class interests. In this way Christianity altered its character. From being originally a movement of the exploited it became the support of the exploiters. A further stage in the decline of primitive Christianity occurred when from being a prescribed religion it became legitimate, even the official religion of the state.

Today it is widely recognized by the evangelical church that the close connection between throne and altar, which developed after Constantine, was not without disadvantages, because the Church was faced with new commitments, considerations and extraneous duties. But the development of Western Christianity cannot be judged solely from the standpoint of present-day knowledge, but must be considered in relation to the times. Moreover, there is a difference between judging the Church from the standpoint of the Gospel and from that of an atheism which is hostile to any form of Christianity and is itself advocating a state system built on an atheistic foundation.

It is true that the history of the Church in the East and the West has not always been a good advertisement for the Gospel, but sometimes just the opposite is true. Here modern Christianity has a great deal to do in the way of sorting out and apportioning the share of guilt for the mistakes of the past. But to demand from the Christianity of past centuries things which have only been recognized in the last few decades is to ask the impossible and to judge unjustly. What befalls the Church and where it has failed can only be judged objectively by the Gospel itself.

5. The Person of Jesus Christ is neither affected nor defeated by Atheistic Criticism

In the literature of materialistic atheism produced during the last hundred years there is not one single attempt in any way to do justice to the person of Jesus Christ as portrayed in the New Testament. That is due not only to atheistic prejudice but also to the historical-materialistic thesis which postulates the masses as the creators of history and refuses to admit the important influence of any one individual personality. Materialistic-atheistic criticism can with justice find fault in many ways with Christians and their history, but the Church and Christians do not live autonomous lives, but live by the word and deeds of Jesus Christ, a figure exalted above criticism. He alone is the centre of the Church and the content of the Christian faith, and already the one-time opponents of Jesus and the powerful figures of the then existing world have had to learn that he whom they killed was raised again from the dead.

II · Reflections on an Evangelical Answer

5 · Materialistic Atheism as seen by the Christian Faith

MATERIALISTIC ATHEISM DOES NOT APPEAR TO THE Christian faith as a uniform entity, but as an agglomeration of opinions and motives, which are not restricted either to a particular part of the world or to any particular group of people. The ultimate decision between faith and unbelief is made in the heart of each individual. Hence a firm distinction must be drawn between the atheism arising from the kind of person one is, or from the circumstances of daily life, and which produces a sense of guilt and remorse, and the atheism which consciously and deliberately cultivates and even boasts of its godlessness.

Besides materialistic atheism, which exalts matter as the ultimate basis of existence, there is also an idealistic form of atheism, which because of its ostensible closeness to theism is a more dangerous adversary of the Christian faith. Alongside theoretical atheism, which makes the conscious rejection of God the basis of its whole interpretation of life, there is a sort of practical atheism, which orders its actual mode of living according to purely immanent mundane factors and behaves as if there were no God.

Modern materialistic atheism is not the invention of the lower social strata, but had its strongest roots and found its most powerful stimulus in the so-called upper strata of society: consider for example the middle-class materialists and atheists of eighteenth-century France. The book *Scientific Outlook* (*Wissenchaftliche Weltanschauung*) rightly points out in relation to the religious criticism of the Young Hegelians that the ideological conflict with religion was not begun by the Marxists, but historically was in origin an essential constituent of the struggle of the rising middle class against feudalism.[1] Of course it is still to be explained why the Marxists, who usually dissociate themselves so vigorously from the middle class, took over and developed precisely this religious-polemical aspect of the bourgeoisie.

The basic difference between the pre-Christian or the extra-Christian atheism, which denied God as the creator, and the post-Christian and anti-Christian atheism, which remains always hostile to the Father of Jesus Christ, must be carefully kept in mind. The various stages of development of this post-Christian atheism need careful analysis and separate evaluation.

Materialistic Atheism as Rebellion against the Living God

Present-day materialistic atheism, as far as its religious polemic is concerned, is to a great extent perpetuating the ancient Promethean rebellion against the living God. Nobody has seen this so clearly and expressed it so definitely as Ludwig Feuerbach. Its motive, man's self-assertion and self-glorification, can be traced back to the beginning of the human race. Feuerbach's influence on materialistic atheism has been and still is very great.

The philosophical starting point for materialistic atheism is not a scientifically established premiss, an irrefutable basic axiom, but a deliberate prior decision, an intellectual prejudice: 'I do not want to be God's creature, but my own maker. I want to owe my existence to myself alone.' The philosophical cloak assumed by materialistic atheism cannot conceal the fact that ultimately it is based on a deliberately chosen attitude: 'It shall not be and must not be God, to whom I owe myself and the world: he simply shall not exist.' Natural man's independence, self-exaltation and self-assertion is intensified into hatred of God, glorification of matter and the apotheosis of man. This phenomenon of the Promethean revolt against God in materialistic atheism can only be studied indirectly by trying to understand the anti-theistic climate through relevant statements. Then it becomes clear that the repeated assertions that there is no God, that science has proved

[1] *Wissenschftliche Weltanschauung*, II 1, Berlin 1960, p. 33.

that God does not exist, and the proofs that have been brought forward, are rooted in a deliberate ontological prejudice and not in any scientifically established principle or the result of any scientific research. In this connection such statements may be cited as: 'The materialist exalts the knowledge of matter and nature, and throws God on to the rubbish heap together with all the philosophers who defend him.' 'Down with God! Long live nature!'[1] In similar vein: 'Therefore Prometheus proclaims that the race that he creates in his image will no longer care about God' (*Unser Deutschland*, p. 129). This is clearly intended to include the Christian God also.

Atheism as the Presupposition, Validation and Result of a Materialistic Outlook

To the founders and champions of materialistic atheism it was clear from the start that in denying the existence of God, in rejecting the creation and the over-ruling power of God, they faced the difficult task of finding a scientific explanation of the world in terms of itself. Logically the onus of proof rests on them. Atheism does not rely solely on the denial of God, but attempts to prove its atheistic ontology, to describe positively and explain its view of 'a world without God', its atheistic doctrine of man. Materialistic atheism is indeed rebellion against God, but it is not content with that; it assumes the task of working out a philosophy of life which is not atheistic by chance but by necessity, not incidentally but essentially. Without losing the element of deliberate choice materialistic atheism attempts in the sphere of philosophy a logically clarified explication of its atheistic principles.

These principles were put forward by Marx and Engels, worked out by Lenin and systematized by Stalin. The best general guide to these principles is the short summary, *Dialectical Materialism* (*Der dialektische Materialismus*, Leipzig 1957) by R. O. Gropp. In contrast to Stalin he deals first with the material nature of the world and then goes on to expound materialistic dialectics.

The materialistic and dialectical principles do not immediately reveal the atheistic character of this philosophy. Further deductive

[1] Lenin, *Aus dem philosophischen Nachlass*, p. 90.

investigation is necessary in order to discover its atheistic roots. The philosophical questions involved are extremely difficult. It will be sufficient to point out here that the scientific view of the world put forward by materialistic atheism is not derived from the actually existing world as data, but from definite philosophical presuppositions, which have not been subjected to proof, but simply accepted as 'given'. According to Stalin's book *Dialectical and Historical Materialism* (*Über dialektischen und historischen Materialismus*, 1938) these presuppositions are: Nature is a coherent homogeneous whole. Nature is a condition of ceaseless movement and change. Evolution is transition from quantitative to qualitative changes. The conflict of opposites is the central element in the process of evolution.

Alongside these main features of the dialectical method the fundamental ideas of philosophical materialism are indicated: The world is by nature material; it develops according to the laws of motion of matter and needs no 'world spirit'. Matter is primary, the original; mind is secondary and derivative. The world and its system of laws are completely comprehensible. Our knowledge is reliable knowledge and there is nothing incomprehensible in the world.

For the Christian faith the basis of atheistic philosophy is no more than a hypothesis resting on the assumption that the existence of God can be disproved by scientific means and that belief in God can be explained by purely natural processes.

The witness of the Bible however, and also some features of non-Christian religions, provide the clearest indication that God is not presented to us like another kind of object, but that in his personal quality (even that is only an approximate picture) he transcends rational-logical and empirical-inductive methods of understanding and appears as the absolute sovereign Lord, who reveals himself or conceals himself in anger or in love. In order to get round this free sovereign character of the living God materialistic atheism proclaimed a concept of science in complete and conscious antagonism to God. Here it might seem as if ultimately an atheistic conviction was set against a theistic faith, and that it was simply this conflict between faith and conviction that had to be considered and resolved. But this is not the case. For it can be shown that materialistic atheism in its scientific outlook suffers from hypertrophy of its own principles. In a medical-biological sense hypertrophy is the abnormal enlargement of an organ or tissue due to exaggerated growth of constituent cells. In an analogical sense one can speak of hypertrophied rationalism, materialism and humanism, meaning by this an exaggerated reliance on reason, matter and humanity, rather in the sense of Lenin's statement: 'The materialist exalts the knowledge of matter, nature. . . .'[1]

Over-estimation of Reason, Matter and Man by Materialistic Atheism

Materialistic atheism is based on the three principles: dialectics, materialism and humanism. There is no doubt that these comprise essential elements and methods of human understanding, organization and social behaviour, and that they have a justifiable though limited claim to recognition. But materialistic atheism gives them an importance far beyond their capabilities, and this not with the aim of establishing the world as a self-contained system and man as autonomous, 'on his own'. Its aim is to undermine faith, discredit religion and refute the existence of God.

The rational investigation of the world is a recognized and necessary human activity, but the efforts of rationalism to understand and explain everything rationally, and its insistence that it is possible to do so, continually encounters the danger of claiming total and absolute authority for reason, and so developing into hypertrophy. Misuse of reason does not invalidate its proper use, but misuse by exaggeration tempts to inadmissible overstepping of limitations and results in false judgments. That is not agnosticism or scepticism, but simply the result of critical realistic thinking.

Materialistic atheism believes in the principle: There is nothing incomprehensible in the world, but no doubt there are things not yet understood, and these will be discovered and explained by the power of science and experiment. This principle contains an assertion and a prediction. The assertion that there is nothing incomprehensible in the world is an expression of opinion incapable

[1] Lenin, *Aus dem philosophischen Nachlass*, p. 90.

of proof, and which cannot be made legitimately in this absolute form. The prediction that things not yet understood will be explained is still less logically cogent or empirically convincing. What does emerge from the statement and the prediction is a rational optimism, which can hardly stand up to sober examination. The same criticism can be made of the statement that Marxism is omnipotent because it is true. The judgment that it is true is a subjective judgment based on a point of view and not on scientific proof, and it is precisely this philosophical basis of Marxism, i.e. atheism, that is controversial and impossible to prove. The power and strength of Marxism is no doubt considerable and is related to the power politics of the world set-up, but that it is omnipotent will be more difficult to establish and is contrary to actual experience. Even the most convinced materialistic atheist will not be able to sustain that assertion, if he seriously considers the limitations of the natural laws and cognitive processes to which we as human beings are subject.

Engels expressed the principle of explaining the world from within itself in this way: 'The materialistic view of natural science is nothing more than the simple understanding of nature just as it is, without any extraneous embellishments.'[1] But the simple understanding of nature 'just as it is, without any embellishments' provides us with impressions and nothing else.

Materialistic atheism is not just hypertrophied rationalism, but also hypertrophied materialism. On this point also Lenin made the classic statement that the materialist exalted the knowledge of matter, of nature. Here properties and capabilities are attributed to matter which cannot be substantiated by objective observation of nature alone. When Walter Hollitscher described in his book, *Evolution in the Universe* (*Die Entwicklung im Universum*, Berlin 1951) a self-contained evolution from the nebulae, through the beginnings of life and the evolution of man, up to the classless society of the future, confining himself mainly to factors inherent in matter itself, he painted an impressive picture, but at the same time he overlooked the interaction of internal and external causes. In modern theories of matter priority is given to internal causes

[1] Engels, *Ludwig Feuerbach*, p. 79.

within matter itself—'self-movement', in contrast to external causes. This means of course that the position of mechanical materialism and the '*milieu*' theory have been discredited, but at the same time a new difficulty has been produced, for now it would have to be explained whence and why the original matter, e.g. in the nebulae, acquired the force and direction for its evolution into life and human beings. In the relevant literature the expression often occurs, without explanation or evidence, that this or that 'developed' into the other. The term 'development' must in this case conceal factors which are of course demonstrable as existing, but the origin of which has not yet been scientifically explained. Thus 'development' becomes a fetish, a *deus ex machina*, that is supposed to explain all the phenomena of the existing world. In this sense materialistic atheism is pure materialism, since it tries to deduce absolutely everything from matter. That is not affected in any way by the fact that in other places other terms are substituted for the 'creation of the material world'. For instance we find nature as the creator, or time, or in Engels' classic phrase 'work created man'. A careful analysis of all the relevant statements shows a firmly rooted belief in the creative capacity of matter.

Finally materialistic atheism is hypertrophied humanism. In this connection Alfred Kurella seems to have said the last word in his book *Man His Own Creator* (*Der Mensch als Schöpfer seiner selbst*, Berlin 1958). Man as creator of himself? Man as creator of God? Here the issue is clear, namely the atheistic hypertrophy of man. But this is only possible when an essential part of reality is overlooked or suppressed, namely everything that was there before man came into existence.

But this idea of man as his own creator is not the final result but the starting point of one single line of western thought beginning in ancient Greece, mythologically with Prometheus, historically with Euhemeros, and religio-philosophically with the sophist Protagoras (480-410 BC), who was accused of atheism because of what he wrote about the gods: 'I know nothing of the gods, neither whether they exist nor whether they do not.' The main tenet of his philosophy is: 'Man is the measure of all things, as to what is and what is not.' Thus any universally valid truth is impossible; everything is relative to man. In the case of Protagoras it is clear that hypertrophied humanism leads to anthropocentricity, positivism and subjective idealism.

What is here understood by hypertrophied humanism can best be illustrated by statements of the classic representatives of materialistic atheism. Karl Marx says: 'Since in the socialist view all world history is nothing but the story of man as the product of human labour, and the development of nature for man, he has a clear and irresistible proof of his birth through his own efforts and of his mode of origin.'[1] Engels also maintains that man created himself by his own labour. This anthropocentric element has not been lost even in modern materialistic atheism. For example, Hermann Duncker (1874-1960) said in a speech on 4th November, 1957 in Berlin: 'Every materialist who aims at being honest and logical cannot but be an atheist. "Atheist" is a purely negative word. It means that we reject the idea of God, but it does not go so far as to say what we put as positive in its place. I believe that it is possible to speak eloquently about atheism without even using the word "atheism", for we can make it clear to our hearers, to young people, that they believe in humanity, in the development of man, and that man can and will understand everything and in his development can achieve everything necessary for the progress of society. It is this faith in humanity that we put in place of belief in God. We must make this consciousness of humanity strong and vigorous in men, because it is at once the foundation of human solidarity, of the sense of belonging together, and so also the realization by all of the necessity for world peace.'[2]

The interesting thing about this statement is that there is no mention of knowledge of humanity but only of faith in it, and that this faith is not acquired but assumed. Some of the original starting points of Marxism—the emphasis on rationality as against irrationality, the recognition of the importance of the concrete as against the abstract, the need to rescue men from the domination of purely material values—would be approved by the Christian faith. Conflict only arises when reason, matter and man are regarded

---

[1] Marx-Engels, *Kleine ökonomische Schriften*, Berlin 1955, p. 139.
[2] *Deutsche Lehrerzeitung*, 23/11/1957.

in isolation as absolutes, and thus interpreted against the reality of God. This threefold hypertrophy assumes that the world has been explained once and for all by materialistic atheism. Against these exaggerated claims it must be urged that there are objective limitations to reason, matter and man, which are impassable and always will be. To deny that is to take refuge in illusion and utopianism. There are objective limits even in the abstract sciences, in Mathematics and Logic. The problem of squaring the circle and the projection of a sphere on to a flat surface approach the limits of rational possibility of representation and demonstrability. The existence and meaning of time are still unexplained; even within materialistic atheism there is hesitation whether time is to be considered absolute (e.g. Victor Stern)[1] or relative. Time can neither be reversed nor repeated. On account of this structure of time historical events are unique, concrete and individual, and at best admit of analogies that are of controversial significance, but no more. The past cannot be reconstructed and so cannot be fully explained. The present is always only experienced in part and is never seen as a whole, not even subsequently. We cannot calculate precisely the consequences of our actions. Scientific prediction has narrow limits.

The fact that it is possible to discover scientific laws of organic nature does not mean that we can also influence them. Thus there are objective limits to exaggerated activism and this is where any belief in human omnipotence founders. Even Stalin in his last book (1952) made a distinction between attainable knowledge and the practical impossibility of influencing inorganic processes: 'To influence astronomical, geological and some other analogous processes is actually beyond the power of men, even when they have understood their laws of development.'[2]

As the representatives of materialistic atheism themselves admit, there is thus a boundary between understanding and the scope of effective action. Even the mere understanding of inorganic

---

[1] Victor Stern (d. 1958) in his book, *Epistemological Problems of Modern Physics* (Berlin 1952), supported the idea of absolute space and time. On this subject a lively discussion was carried on from the beginning of 1953 till the middle of 1956 in the *Deutsche Zeitschrift für Philosophie*.

[2] Stalin, *Economic Problems of Socialism in the USSR*, Moscow 1952, p. 6.

processes is limited. This limitation is obviously not due to the incapacity of reason, but to the character of the continually changing and never completely observable subject. Understanding, explanation and the power to influence lie on different levels. The possibilities of experimentation are limited by differences of space and time. There are spheres in which experiment and repetition are impossible and progress is only possible by dangerous ventures. A detailed picture of the world as it is cannot be given in one plane. There are differences of space and time, differences in quality of being, and varying relationships to man. The inorganic world, the organic world of animals and the world of men are not only related as matter but are also differentiated by reasons of specific new laws to which they are subject. Human society cannot, as Stalin asserted, be understood as exactly as biology, because it is much more complex.

In the Christian faith the recognition of the limitations of reason, matter and humanity does not lead to resignation or scepticism, as materialistic atheism fears. Instead the Christian sees his duty in the need of the moment, in the particular circumstances as obedience to God, who has placed us men in a finite and limited world.

Materialistic Atheism becomes a Creed, Apotheosis and Cult

Materialistic atheism does not confine itself to the denial of God and the exposition of its scientific view of the world, but through its rationalistic, materialistic and humanistic hypertrophy develops towards a religious cult. In its dispute with idealism and religion it likes to be regarded as a view of the world based only on philosophy and science, because it understands the fascination exercised nowadays by everything labelled 'science', and so it sets itself up as the opponent of 'superstition', 'mysticism', 'obscurantism' and 'clericalism'. This black and white terminology is intended to make it easy for the reader, especially if he is uneducated and inexperienced, to decide in favour of and support the alleged right side. But even the more elaborate phraseology used in putting forward the alternatives of theism and atheism present a simple choice, for example when the alternatives are presented as scientific assumptions as against religious prejudice, or freedom as against religious bondage. Both kinds of phraseology, the simple and the more elaborate, lead back to the ultimate antithesis—in the sense understood by materialistic atheism—of science (knowledge) and faith. And here in this fundamental analysis everything depends of course on what is understood on the one side by 'science' and on the other by 'faith'.

Looking at materialistic atheism in its simplified philosophical form, the Christian faith finds argument difficult, because the atheistic character of the philosophical premisses and deductions is not immediately apparent. The distinction between faith and atheism becomes clearer and more definite in those places already indicated as examples of threefold hypertrophy. But the antithesis between faith and atheism becomes clearest where atheism has been reduced to a creed (a confession of faith), and apotheosis and a cult.

In the conflict with idealism, religion and faith materialistic atheism prefers to argue from its own philosophical basis, and avoids bringing in the elements of hypertrophy and cult. But both hypertrophy and cult are involved, and so the Christian faith is justified in taking them into consideration in forming a judgment. The Christian faith is interested not only in the philosophical basis of materialistic atheism but also in its creed, apotheosis and cult, because it is here that the element of faith appears in atheism more clearly than in philosophical argument.

The Christian faith is interested firstly in the atheistic creed. It is clear from the early writings of Marx and Engels that their spiritual and philosophical struggle had been ultimately a matter of religion and theology up till the forties of the last century. It was then that Cabet (1788-1856) produced his *Communist Creed* (*Crédo communiste*), which in the following year (1842) was translated into German by Lorenz von Stein. In 1847 Karl Schapper (1813-1870) and Josef Moll (1812-1849) sent to the 'friends on the continent' a new confession of faith in the form of a catechism, for their approval. At the end of 1847 Karl Marx was working on the draft of a communist confession of his own, but Engels suggested the term 'manifesto' instead of 'confession' and

the abandonment of the idea of a catechism. This was done. None
the less in materialistic atheistic circles the term 'faith' is in
common use—faith in reason, in history, in technology, in the
ability and strength of man. It is this broadening of materialistic
atheism's scientific view of life beyond objective reality into the
sphere of faith that provides the real area of conflict and the true
criterion of judgment.

It can also be established that in materialistic atheism there are
elements of apotheosis. In the experience of the Christian faith
it is a tragic law of human nature that separation from God leads
to the deification of material things and values, which it is ultimately impossible to check. The hypertrophy becomes religious.
The truth of this experience is confirmed by the story of materialistic atheism, beginning with Feuerbach, when he started off by
denying the creation of the world and of man, and eventually
went so far as to say: 'Man created God in his own image.' Marx
and Engels were realistic enough to keep clear of this apotheosis,
this deification of human things and values. But Marx nevertheless
gave a pointer towards apotheosis when he said: 'The more a man
relies on God, the less of himself he retains.' For here one could
say just the opposite: The more a man relies on himself and the
world, the less remains for God. But a man who has banished God
from himself and the world cannot endure a godless world and
creates new gods for himself. That is the ontological reason why
hypertrophy develops into apotheosis.

The path from hypertrophy to apotheosis can be traced through
definite stages, beginning with the statement of the Frenchman
Raynal (1713-1796) who was at first a parson then later a historian:
'Peoples of the world! If you would be free, break down all the
altars and destroy all the thrones.'[1]

Feuerbach, the great destroyer, takes refuge in the religion of
love and devotes himself to that. Marx declares that man is the
supreme being and Engels speaks of the certainty that matter in
all its transformations remains always the same. Marx rightly saw
that the subordination of man to capital and material possessions
leads to his being dehumanized, which it was his life's aim to

---

[1] Johannes Scherr, *Die Hexe von Glarus*, Berlin 1952, p. 229.

prevent. But is it not true that man cannot endure being alone, and willingly and of necessity gives up his independence and tries to find something firm and durable to give his heart to, something that will provide him with stability and relieve him as far as possible of responsibility? But this is the decisive question: To whom is he to give his heart—to God or to man, to things and ideas?

Where belief in God has been given up, the way is open to apotheosis, even to the deification of man. Alfons Goldschmidt in *How I rediscovered Moscow* (1925) describes the effect of the death of Lenin thus: 'Our hearts flew up into the communist heaven—to Lenin. For Lenin is surely sitting up there. He has become the great father, who from heaven guides the earth, which is indeed the function of a heavenly father. Lenin is glorified. Below on earth everything that he has said and written is being collected. The Newest Testament is being written, edited and annotated. In Russia the Old Testament has ceased to count, although there are still millions who pray and feel according to the Old and New Testaments: it is the Newest Testament that matters. It is no longer a divine testament but the legacy of a great father, who in his lifetime represented the will of the people, a will which death only made clearer and more universal, but did not change.' 'Every great father is a father by destiny, and only reflects the light given to him. He is produced by the dynamic of progress. He is always first a prophet, then a hero, then a tangible god and then an idea.'[1] In the same year, 1924, Alfred Kerr wrote in similar vein: 'This dead man will always rise again, in a hundred forms, till justice rules the chaos of the world.'[2]

The idea of resurrection is developed by Johannes R. Becher through the idea of awakening: 'The people have spoken. Stalin has carried out Lenin's testament and awakened him from death.' The same poet, J. R. Becher, expressed this idea in other words: 'Your name lives for ever,' and 'In our new life the life of Stalin lives eternally.' On the 6th March, 1953, the day after Stalin's death, the poet Arnold Zweig produced an astronomical variation

---

[1] *Er rührte an den Schlaf der Welt*, Berlin 1954, p. 47f.
[2] *Op. cit.*, p. 70.

of the idea of immortality at an improvised memorial ceremony at
Oberhof: 'Although we shall never forget that Stalin was a living
man, who loved the future and its children, who was rough and
without sentimentality, yet he will be gradually transformed into
a star, like the evening star now shining through our darkness.'
The poet Bodo Uhse gave the idea a philosophical-historical
significance by saying about Stalin, 'He dealt with all problems
and each one of his words determined the course of history.'

How the godless world inevitably leads back to the very myth
it set out to combat can be seen in the mythological hymn composed by the poet Stephan Hermlin as a lament on the death of
Stalin: 'It is said that at the news of Stalin's death the lights of
Moscow began to go out, as though by a mysterious common
consent. Then the lights of the trams went out also. . . . The same
generation, which was granted the good fortune to live at a time
when the world is changing finally and irrevocably, in which man
is beginning to realize his destiny, and in which across the graves
of those who sacrificed their lives for the liberation of mankind
land after land is becoming a stronghold of reason, a time in which
Stalin marched at the head of five continents—this same generation
has now had to suffer the loss of Stalin.'[1]

The statements quoted above need to be considered in their
intended historical philosophical-religious aspect. It is a remarkable fact that materialistic atheism, which likes to consider itself
a science, should find itself on the way to becoming a creed,
apotheosis and cult. Individual exact sciences may indeed have a
tendency to extend their objective view of reality into a total view,
and so to expand their particular picture of the world into a
general philosophy, but still they hesitate to let their objective and
immanent points of view venture into the field of religion, or to
become the basis of a cult. The exceptions—possibly biologism
or historicism (Haeckel, H. St. Chamberlain)—only confirm the
rule.

But materialistic atheism has already gone a long way along the
road to becoming a cult. Within its own circles it speaks of the

[1] Quotations from Becher, Zweig, Uhse and Hermlin in *Du Welt im Licht*,
Berlin 1954.

cult of labour as the only possible cult. Its philosophy, consisting mainly of scientific elements, is extended into the field of religious cult. Its ideas acquire concrete visible forms, and there are 'sacred things' that are revered and claim the service of men. The events in human life that are particularly susceptible to this—birth, going to school, leaving school, puberty, marriage and death, are not only brought into the materialistic-atheistic view of the world, but are also interpreted ethically and presented in the form of a cult. This is not just an imitation of church customs and usages or the expression of 'pseudo-religion' or 'pseudo-church', but corresponds to a general human desire for concrete representation, devotion and submission. Atheistic free-thinking funeral celebrations had been in existence for a long time, particularly in the case of cremation, then in 1954 the youth dedication ceremonies were revived, a custom underlined in 1959 by the issue of special postage stamps. Recently socialist christenings or child-dedication ceremonies have been added, which in one case at least, at Stalinstadt, were described as atheistic baptism. Since 1958 there have also been socialist marriages celebrated by state officials. In the case of child-dedication and marriage the participating adults were required to take a vow to give their children a socialist upbringing.

This development into creed, apotheosis and cult must be seen against a background of a total materialistic-atheistic view of life, which claims to answer all questions and extends to all areas of life. Recently in July 1958 after years of discussion of socialist morality, an ethical element has been added to the cult form by the 'Ten Commandments of Socialist Ethics and Morals', from which it is clearly evident that after materialistic atheism had given a forthright 'No' to traditional truths and values, it was forced to recognize that man cannot live on a 'No', and that an ideal society could not be built on a contradiction alone, but that man needs a fixed point, a clear 'Thou shalt'. Even if the wording of the socialist commandments does not bear an obviously atheistic stamp, the number (ten) of the commandments and the form 'Thou shalt' is reminiscent of the Hebrew-Christian decalogue, and it is evident from the general sense that a supreme value created by man himself is intended as a substitute for the first commandment of the decalogue, because man is deliberately taking entirely into his own hands the planning of his personal and social life.

Materialistic Atheism as a Protest against the Guilt of the Church and Christianity

Materialistic atheism is rebellion against the living God and welcomes anything that can be used to support its position. Consequently its picks out whatever aspects of the history of the Church can be cited as evidence of guilt, injustice and uncharitableness. It recasts this criticism with not always unjustifiable passion and violence into an often understandable protest. In this it claims to speak in the name of humanity, life and reason, and encourages corresponding wishes and desires, in order that it may itself point the way to freedom and prosperity. Actually both motives, rebellion against God and the protest against the guilt of Christianity, are seldom completely worked out, but overlap and confuse each other. But in order to form a fair and accurate judgment the theoretical distinction between them is possible and necessary.

The understandable urge to protest against the guilt and shortcomings of the Church and Christianity gives materialistic atheism strength, purpose and a relatively good conscience. It gives the great words freedom, dignity, humanity, prosperity, peace and happiness their firm place in atheistic writings, and by skilful presentation can arouse great passion and produce considerable effect: The world must be made better. Man must be born again. In this respect the efforts of materialistic atheism are often ingenious, accurate and sincere.

Honesty, justice and love demand that Christianity should face the past squarely, even if it is painful (Ps. 32.4f). But it should not stop at vague references to the failure of the Church; it must also examine the criterion by which the criticism is made. Failure on the part of the Church and Christianity can only be seen where they have been faithless to their own task, where they have spoken and acted contrary to their own principles. What is their real guilt in the light of the Gospel? Here a final judgment can only be pronounced by the Word and in the heart, as we are made to realize that we are at once the judges and the judged.

Now let us examine some of the charges that materialistic atheism levels at the Church and Christianity.

The fact that wealthy people accepted Christianity and that it became reconciled to the Roman state is held to be a defection from the original form of Christianity. It is contended that ever since then the Church has been on the side of the rich and often against the poor. The bloody persecution of heretics and its mistaken attitude to science (e.g. Copernicus, Galileo, Bruno, Servetus and others) are particularly sore points, and closely allied is the question of verbal inspiration and the biblical view of the world. The evil consequences of the Inquisition are described vividly and at length.

The modern gulf between East and West is ascribed to the injustice committed by western Christianity against the eastern, when the Pope of Rome excommunicated the Metropolitan of Constantinople in 1054. The tragic entanglements of the Peasants' Revolt in Germany, with which Luther and Münzer were associated, have done serious harm to the cause of the Gospel. The fact that the social problems that broke out with great fury in the nineteenth century were not taken seriously enough by the Church still has serious consequences today. In some European countries (France and Russia) the churches owned a great deal of property, which was more of a handicap to them internally and externally than a means to freedom and service. Materialistic atheism even reproaches the Church for making pronouncements in the field of science and other branches of knowledge in which it has no expertise, and conversely for remaining silent in the face of injustice.

In this connection recent atheistic literature provides a means of assessment and a warning sign. This literature tries to prove the failure of Christianity all along the line. For this it digs out suitable material from the obscurity of archives and the murk of history and presents it to the public. Nor has the horizon been limited to Europe. Other nations and the history of the earliest times have been brought in, as in the case of the establishment of the atheistic tradition. The result may well contain a good deal of exaggeration, distortion and misunderstanding, but the Christian faith is bound to take seriously the matter raised by materialistic atheism.

The part of the argument that materialistic atheism tries to base on philosophy and the atheistic tradition is illustrated in the general atheistic literature by concrete examples. In this it does not confine itself to recent productions, but includes any works in foreign languages and material from the distant past and far-away countries which may serve its purpose—to defeat any form of faith. In this it is obviously following the advice of Engels (1874) and Lenin (1922) 'to translate and distribute widely among the people the polemical atheistic literature from the end of the eighteenth century'.[1] In accordance with this advice a new edition of the French atheists of the eighteenth century was called for and quickly put in preparation. An incomplete survey shows that the works of authors in many languages are represented, French, English and American, Italian, Spanish and Portuguese, Swedish, Flemish, Czech and Polish. The recently issued works of older writers like Diderot (1713-1784), Manzoni (1785-1873), Queiroz (1843-1900) and Jacobsen (1874-1885), whose novel *Niels Lyhne* was described as the Bible of atheism, are mostly witty and ironic, often border on the pornographic, but offer at times not wholly unjustified criticism. In contrast the new production of literary works with an atheistic slant in the German language is mostly very thin in form and content.

Not in every case but in many criticism of the Church is the main theme. It is chiefly the Catholic Church that comes under fire, particularly in regard to its influence in the past, in the Far East and in everyday life. It is accused of uncharitableness and falsehood. Descriptions of defection from the Christian faith are popular and are claimed as conversions to atheism. References to personal development based on experience and education are more or less superficial and cling to fortuitous experience, mostly in youth. There is complete absence of any serious discussion of the Christian faith at its deeper level. In general what is presented as Christianity in most of these writings is shocking and shameful. There is not a scrap of understanding of faith and the Church,

[1] Marx-Engels, *On Religion*, p. 141; Lenin, *Religion*, p. 37.

and one wonders whether there is any desire at all to understand and describe the Christian faith. Nevertheless under the charges of human failure on the part of the Christian faith, selfishness, harshness, injustice and falsehood, there is a real need for repentance. For even in human conduct the truth and goodness of God have to be shown forth. The atheist forms his picture of the Christian faith from his experience of individual Christians. It is from them that he forms his idea of what the Christian is called to demonstrate in his daily life. Hence even the often unfounded criticism of the Christian faith in atheistic literature should be a call to Christians to a holy way of life in the faith, even though the most righteous conduct may not convince the unbelievers.

Materialistic Atheism as a Temptation to the Church and the Christian Faith

Seen from the Christian angle materialistic atheism has a further function to fulfil. If it is true, as Christians believe, that God is Lord of history, time and nations, then materialistic atheism also has a place in God's plan of judgment and salvation. God permits it and uses it for his own purpose. Christianity should consider carefully and constantly the significance of materialistic atheism for itself. Is it a judgment and a visitation? Is it a temptation and a challenge?

One thing is not possible—to draw a line dividing the Christian faith from materialistic atheism between the two contemporary politically and ideologically conditioned halves of the world, as though the West were Christian and the East atheist. The boundary does not run between groups of people but right through the heart of each individual, including the Christian. There is no neutral zone completely outside the power of God, but neither is there a citadel completely free from the challenge of atheism. The Christian who imagines himself to be exalted beyond the reach of materialistic atheism has already succumbed to it.

The most obvious form of atheism is where a man accepts the atheistic view of life and surrenders to it, and believes that he has to fight against God. But not only atheism but even disbelief in God is a denial of him. A man is an atheist in the broader sense when he places his ultimate confidence in some earthly power and relies more on human means of security than on the word and the promises of God. As Luther said, whatever a man gives his heart to, whether to the living God or to some earthly power and values, that is the criterion for belief or unbelief.

Materialistic atheism is such a serious temptation to the Christian faith because it recognizes the tangible, visible and demonstrable as the basis of existence, and commends science as the means of controlling fate and for the determination of the future. Materialistic atheism goes for the obvious, for what can be seen. What church, what Christian is not tempted by the earthly power and security that is always being offered to them so easily and seductively? Besides that there are inherent difficulties in the Christian faith itself, namely that there are no specific directions in the Bible relative to the modern situation, so that there is no universally convincing way of applying generally accepted norms to a concrete situation. Then too it remains doubtful how far a decision binding on a Christian is also binding on others. A further difficulty is that there are no unequivocable indications, so that in matters of faith there is always an element of venture.

It is just when living by faith (Heb. 11.1) is taken seriously, namely as enduring hope in ultimate salvation and trust in the invisible truth of faith, that the seduction of materialistic atheism, with its emphasis on the immediately tangible, becomes apparent. In so much as materialistic atheism claims to base itself and its attitude on something tangible it is seductive and tempting. Every period in the history of the Church has had its specific and concrete temptations, and every generation of believers has had to overcome special susceptibilities and the possibility of defection —e.g. David Friedrich Strauss, Feuerbach, Nietzsche, Haeckel, the race myth—and in each generation fellow Christians have fallen by the way. Our generation has been given materialistic atheism as the ordeal by fire, and so it is part of the picture of the Church in the twentieth century.

The temptation of Christianity by materialistic atheism has of course its special character, that must not be over-simplified by a superficial classification into practical and theoretical atheism.

An essential part of the temptation lies in the structure and methods of materialistic atheism itself. It claims that it alone is science and that it possesses the truth exclusively, while everything else is 'superstition', 'mysticism', or 'obscurantism'. This claim and the misrepresentation of the Christian faith can only be countered by the truth of the Gospel.

A more serious temptation however arises from the fact that the structure of materialistic atheism makes it possible to enlist the power of the state, and that it is already well on the way to becoming the official outlook of the state. Refusal to accept the atheistic part of the materialistic view of the world is increasingly interpreted as a reservation with regard to the state itself. It is sad that the power of the state is being widely used to encourage atheism by discrediting the Christian faith and to destroy every form of 'religion'. The methods of publicity are so employed that atheism is brought even to those who do not want it, and the voice of the Church is withheld from those who want to hear it. The conditions relating to literary production are being increasingly interpreted in the direction of atheistic progress and are deprived of their original intention, as atheism is given more and more opportunities and Christianity less and less. The aim seems to be to restrict the Church within the 'freedom of worship,' with the eventual result of cutting off all other forms of activity.

If the question of 'materialistic atheism or the Christian faith' were submitted to the free and responsible judgment of the citizens, and if the Church were allowed to answer with equal freedom every unjustified attack, and if both sides were afforded equal opportunities, which would be democratically quite legitimate in view of the proportion of Christians in the population, then the situation would be wide open and promising, because atheism raises ultimate questions of faith, which the Church could answer at the deepest level. But when the power of the state allies itself with atheistic assumptions, encourages atheism and supports propaganda against the Christian faith, then a serious situation arises for Christians, leading to bitter conflicts. The Church warns believers against defection or opportunist compromise, and seeks in her own way to find a practical line of action. The numerically small and theologically weak group that tries to find a solution in compromise with the socialist social order overlooks the fact that the socialist order is based on atheism and shows no signs of abandoning it. Since socialism sees itself as a total entity, co-operating with it while ignoring its ideological-atheistic basis is not welcomed and is regarded as 'revisionism'. Any division of socialism into an ideological side, which can hardly be supported by the Christian faith, and a social-economic side, which it could accept, is intolerable to socialism, because it insists on being accepted entirely or not at all. Neither socialism nor the state see themselves just as a liberal administrative power or a welfare organization, but lay claim to absolute truth and aim at transforming into complete happiness and prosperity by economic means all the ills of mankind, which it blames on economic conditions.

Christianity and the Church wish to serve by the power of the Gospel and according to the best of their knowledge and conscience those who have lapsed into godlessness.

6 · Materialistic Atheism in Conflict with the Christian Faith

IN THE FOLLOWING PAGES AN ATTEMPT IS MADE TO SET out some considerations suggesting an evangelical answer to materialistic atheism. It is an experiment rather than a final pronouncement. First a few lines of thought will be developed which compel the Church to pay attention to materialistic atheism and find an answer.

Where the Church should listen to Materialistic Atheism

For Christians and the Church the acknowledgment of the triune God is finally conclusive, as it has been since Christianity began. Here atheism and faith stand in irreconcilable opposition. The Christian faith knows and confesses that God, the Creator and Lord of the world, is also the Lord of the nations and states and controls their destiny till the day of judgment. Such a faith has the freedom and the duty to inquire how materialistic atheism regards the Christian faith and the Church, and what its functions can be in relation to Christianity.

1. The Position of Man in Nature

Materialistic atheism presents the position of natural man, i.e. of man before and apart from the Gospel, most clearly and most starkly: self-consciousness as the supreme deity, man as the highest being, the world as self-contained. This outlook and this onto-logical climate of opinion have found their clearest expression in modern materialistic atheism. Accordingly the Gospel has got to reckon with man, not as a worthy harmless being, but as in contradiction, in rebellion against God. Materialistic atheism's view of existence might be expressed as: We will have nobody over us. We will ourselves be master.

This would preserve the Church and the Christian faith from the illusion that man has a naturally Christian soul that only needs to be cultivated and trained. Man is not like a blank sheet of paper on which you can write what you like. He is possessed and dominated, and the only question is by whom. To realize this is not a natural human endowment, but is the work of the Gospel, which shows man his own situation in relation to God. Thus we are warned by atheism against a false 'Christianizing' of the world. The life of a normal average man guided by his own heart is not God-filled but far removed from him. Thus materialistic atheism shows the Church the need to think seriously about its task, its possibilities and its limitations. Her duty is not to cultivate something old, or to dignify man, but to proclaim something new and beyond our understanding, the voice of God in Christ to men, who without it must perish. Thus materialistic atheism acquires against its will and understanding the function of purifying and refining Christianity.

2. *Other Foundations than the Gospel*

Materialistic atheism has a very sharp eye and a very keen ear for any discordant notes of worldliness or human self-interest in the actual presentation of such ideas as 'religion', 'faith', and 'Christianity'. It must be admitted that the Gospel is seldom exemplified quite purely in any Christian life, and that it may sometimes even be misused to cover very worldly aims. Materialistic atheism often seems able to distinguish the pure tones of genuine faith from the confused sounds of a religion that only serves as a cover for some other aim. Anyone who is only concerned with the Gospel of God for men had best avoid such attempts to misuse the faith for other purposes. Here too atheism can exercise a purifying function for the Church.

But there is something else that must be said. Materialistic atheism thinks that it can get rid of genuine faith in God by looking at it from an ideological angle and drawing conclusions which are far removed from the faith itself. It is pointless to represent every belief and every Christian as serving capitalism. It is indeed the profoundest conviction of Christianity that the Gospel and the Church are ultimately God's affair and not men's, and so serve all men without regard to parties and groups. The proclamation of the Gospel is not intended to help one group and harm another, but offers God's salvation to all men.

Thus materialistic atheism teaches the Church to hold aloof from all attempts to base its task in the world on any other foundation than the Gospel. The readiness with which the Church, by reason of the development of western thought, once adopted as a matter of course the most varied ideas and movements in its support has indeed been missing for several decades.

Philosophical, social and cultural agencies, which the Church has frequently made use of in the past, are breaking down, and so the Church is brought back again to the narrow but firm ground: the word, acts and person of Jesus Christ. By giving up idealism and ontology the Church does not lose anything, as seemed likely at first, but in fact gains, because in the end it finds itself with only one task to fulfil with full authority, namely to testify to the reality of God.

3. Concern about Man

Since the early days of Marxism materialistic atheism has been deeply concerned about man, and this has continued till the present day, although confused and overlaid with other matters. Man is seen in his varied relationships to nature and to society and in his 'involvement' in struggle and labour. Materialistic atheism hopes to prevent man's self-alienation by bringing in a new order of society, so that man will be completely self-contained and on his own. It is when materialistic atheism speaks of man's dereliction and depravity and is concerned for change and renewal that it achieves its greatest depth and approaches nearest and most fruitfully to the Christian faith.

Atheism is aware that man is a social and functional being, and emphasises passionately the need to take seriously his physical and temporal life. It aims not only to understand the world, but above all to change and reform it, not just for the sake of 'activism' but with a definitely humanistic aim. It knows the selfish nature of man and believes it is possible to change it fundamentally by the abolition of private property and the proclamation of common ownership. It knows that man can be delivered over to chaos and despotism and is threatened by annihilation. The forms and theories of materialistic atheism even conceal a deep misgiving about the perilous abysses of life, and at this level the Gospel and atheism are in fruitful tension.

4. *The Dangers of Ideologies*

When the Gospel encounters men who are trying to find security in abstractions and organization, it is often transformed into an ideology—Christian, western, or middle-class. But the Gospel always provides its own insights also and enables men, who allow themselves to be moved by it, to remember what is essential and let the inessential go. Thus the Church is made free to criticize its own past and to consider its responsibility to the future, free at once from the dead weight of the past and free from illusions about the future. Materialistic atheism by its often superficial reproaches forces the Church to work out what is essential and crucial and to penetrate through the artificial alternatives of men to the one essential insight, namely that truth and salvation are only to be found in Jesus Christ. If it is true that for the Gospel atheism is a genuine antithesis, then the Church will be able to learn something from it for her service to the world in the name of God. In comparison with earlier decades, in doctrine and in preaching the Church is becoming more faithful to the Gospel and closer to Christ, but it has still a great deal to learn about charity, kindly living and sympathetic understanding of others however humble.

5. *False Syntheses*

By its conscious and deliberate godlessness materialistic atheism preserves the Church and the Christian from becoming involved with the superficial analogies and premature syntheses, which are sometimes attempted. Materialistic atheism itself is mostly free from such false moods of compromise, but in the no-man's-land between the fronts there are individuals and groups who want the best of both sides, but who are nowhere really at home. The religious attitude to materialistic atheism stands or falls with the question whether atheism is prepared in principle, in areas where it has power and influence, to grant full recognition to believers in the Christian faith and to let them live by it. The solution cannot be found in an accommodation with materialistic atheism, however cunningly supported, unless responsibility is accepted for an abbreviated and truncated Gospel. The crucial statement of beliefs has already been formulated in 1934 in the Barmen Theses. These are fully valid today, in spite of the changes in the nature of the opposition, and they make the ideological basis of any abbreviated theology unacceptable.

6. Belief in God the Central Question

Materialistic atheism, in so far as it is genuine atheism and not just dogmatic materialism, makes the question of belief in God central, particularly for those who have renounced the Church and are outside its influence. In actual fact by continually raising the question of belief in God, although it was decided negatively by Marx and Engels over a hundred years ago, and so was supposed to have been settled, materialistic atheism keeps interest in the Faith and in the Gospel alive in a way that the Church itself could not do. At the same time it forces the Church to consider its fundamental mission and to concentrate on the essentials in its service to the world. And here where freedom of belief and conscience are involved there could be an element of promise.

7. A Reason for the Hope that is in Us

Materialistic atheism sets Christianity yet another task, one already outlined in the First Epistle of St Peter: 'Always be prepared to make a defence to any one who calls you to account for the hope that is in you.' Christianity has testified again and again to the fact of its faith, and to him in whom it believes, and has often disputed more than it should about how it believes. Now, if the signs of the times are not misleading, the great moment has come for it to say to unbelievers and the godless *why* it believes. Materialistic atheism forces Christianity to find the answer, and Christianity has every reason to listen to and to ponder over the question. In the Church also there are tides and opportunities. At the moment there is much talk about the 'changed world', 'the world come of age', and the 'Church for the world', and all this leads to the conclusion that the power of the Spirit can be seen in the Church impelling it to its missionary task in the world. Here materialistic atheism becomes a stimulus, the 'schoolmaster to bring us unto Christ' (Gal. 3.24) in order that the Church may say why it believes.

Although Marx regarded the question of religion as in theory settled, because he considered the truth of religion disproved, the atheistic propaganda, which has steadily revived since 1953, shows quite clearly that more than a hundred years after Marx' rejection of God this question is not settled at all but is still wide open. Indeed the hidden and unintended effect of this atheistic propaganda may actually be to revive and strengthen 'interest in religion'. It is in fact to the credit of materialistic atheism that in its treatment of Christianity it does not restrict itself to superficialities but apart from a few cynical statements, gets down to fundamental questions and so compels the Church and Christians to consider their own position. The Church and Christianity owe a duty to materialistic atheism and its followers to give reasons in chapter and verse why they believe. Christians as fellow-workers with God—neither as functionaries nor priests nor cogs in a machine, but as free and responsible fellow-workers in God's plan of salvation for the world—must convince men by word and deed that they believe not from hypocrisy nor frivolity, nor as a matter of convenience, not even in order to destroy the edifice of socialism, but with sound reasons. That does not mean reducing faith to the level of rationality and so abandoning its essential truth, but it means saying in modern language to the men of today what the disciples and apostles proclaimed to the men of their day: that Jesus is the Christ of God for us men and for our salvation.

It is ominous that in dealing with materialistic atheism the Church is compelled to bear witness to itself, for it has always been quite easy to obtain detailed and reliable information about the Church and the Christian faith, about Christ and the Bible. Unfortunately almost all the statements made by materialistic atheism about church affairs are distorted and inaccurate. There is hardly a single statement from that side that shows the slightest sign of an attempt to understand the real nature of the Christian faith. Many of these false judgments are, as we have already seen, due to the ambiguous way in which Christianity is often presented. A further factor is of course that the majesty and kingdom of Christ are still hidden. Thus there is no alternative left to the Church and to Christians but to bear witness about themselves to materialistic atheism, what they are and what they are trying to do, and also what they are not and what they are not trying to do.

1. Knowledge and Faith

Christianity has always confessed its faith in the triune God in the form of the Apostles' Creed. This faith, in the New Testament sense, and in the meaning understood by the reformed denominations, does not mean an intellectual assent to truth, or a lack of definite knowledge, but expresses a personal relationship, a relationship of trust, love and obedience to the Creator and Ruler of the world. In view of the fact that Christianity confesses that kind of faith in God, many things imputed to the Christian faith by atheistic authors break down.

The Christian faith is not a relationship to things, nor a matter of reason and intellect, i.e. it is not an I-it relationship but I-thou, a relationship of persons. The Christian faith is not so much a question of 'I know' but rather of 'I trust'. Faith in the biblical, 'reformed' sense is not a question of knowing or not knowing, but of something quite different. Knowledge and faith operate at different levels.

Knowledge is a fundamentally different category from faith. Knowledge is objectively and impartially conditioned, and in many cases but not all, can be confirmed by experiment and practice.

Knowledge is distinguishable and at the same time limited by its methods and content. Only such objects as are accessible to men through their senses and their thinking can be the subject of knowledge. Faith and knowledge may indeed be connected, but are not dependent on each other. When knowledge and faith are played off one against the other by materialistic atheism, closer inspection reveals an underlying atheistic presupposition about knowledge and an idealistic misunderstanding about faith, so that the real tension between them is not recognized.

Christian faith is not within men's power to achieve, but is the work of the Holy Spirit. Faith does not rest on idealism but depends on God. It is not a partial function but a total function. Hence every attempt to base faith on something lower, on religion or idealism, is excluded. Unlike philosophy, materialism or idealism faith does not start out from some actual existing material facts and then progress upwards until it eventually reaches the idea of the divine, but it is an affirmative response to the call of God, which comes to me through his word and speaks to my situation here and now. This call of God can find man in the midst of his daily work and thinking.

2. Faith as Personal Relationship

Faith is a personal relationship between Jesus Christ and the believer. Luther's catechism says it in a very simple way: 'I believe that Jesus Christ is my Lord. Belief in the lordship of Jesus Christ over me and over the whole world rests on the manifold and reliable testimony of the Evangelists and Apostles to Jesus of Nazareth as the Christ of God, and on the experience that the words of Jesus contain a call to me here and now.'

3. The Gospel as the Call of God

The Gospel is neither philosophy nor religion. Its content is the proclamation of the kingship of God in Christ, prepared by the Prophets and testified to by the Apostles. Christ is the fulfilment of the promise and at the same time the source and substance of the Gospel. It is not bound up with so-called 'religious' feelings and does not set out to arouse emotion, but works by its own power where the reality and truth of God are known and recognized as God's word and action towards men.

This Gospel is not capable of proof like a material object or a natural law, but demands a decision of personal involvement by acceptance or rejection, indeed with the full weight of the responsibility entailed. Because the Gospel is the compelling call of God to all men, and because the Gospel applies also to atheists, the Church must always insist in every possible way on man's responsibility before God, and must not leave men under the illusion that there is no God.

This Gospel, because of its origin and aims, is inseparable from the person of Jesus of Nazareth, and so cannot be derived from the idea of religion or of idealism, but is fundamentally a completely independent entity. Neither the Gospel nor the Christian faith can be derived from philosophy or history or science, but neither can it be refuted by them. It is possible to examine and describe the origin and content of the Gospel with the aid of historical and other scientific means, if the biblical sources are not approached with hatred of God. However, to understand and accept that God, the Creator of the world, is the Father of Jesus Christ, and so the source of the Gospel, and loves and speaks to every man, is not a matter of human choice, but is the work and fruit of the Holy Spirit.

4. Understanding the Bible

Materialistic atheism has a one-sided and mistaken understanding of the Bible. Prejudice and hostile methods make any real understanding of the Bible impossible, with the result that materialistic atheism shows no sign of any effort to grasp the essential and crucial elements of the Bible, but confines itself to a few passages, often torn from their context, in order to refute the Book of Books.

The Bible as a work of literature is subject to literary-historical laws. Many people known and unknown belonging to many different generations have contributed to its production over a period of about a thousand years. It is a literary monument and the product of a culture, but it is not only that. Towering above all the different meanings found in the Bible and extending from the first page to the last there is always the witness through human lips to God's word and actions. The authority of the Bible stands or falls with the authority of God, who revealed himself first through Moses and the Prophets and then finally once and for all in Jesus Christ. It is an essential part of God's revelation by men and to men that it takes place in the concrete setting of time and place. But all through it the living voice of the Gospel is still to be heard, as it was in the past and will be in the future. H. Fuchss' question, 'Is the Bible right ?' is beside the point. What matters in the Bible is the voice and testimony of God.

5. *Church and Christianity*

The word 'Church' has many meanings and is ambiguous. It contains historical, philosophical, sociological, financial, legal and other aspects. But the innermost nature of the Church cannot be understood from its human relationships, but only from the activity of the Holy Spirit. 'Church' in this sense is not identical with what is usually called Christianity. The word 'Christianity' includes also by-products and waste products of human history, and because of its involvement in the world Christianity is tangled up with many complications and difficulties from the past. But the Church is sustained by sources unknown to other human associations. Its life does not depend on the virtues of its members, nor does it perish because of the vices of those who pay lip service to it. Materialistic atheism still seizes upon a long since outmoded picture of Christianity dating from the turn of the century. Hence its criticism is often concerned with inessentials and is ineffective as far as true believers are concerned.

6. *The Question of the View of the World*

Materialistic atheism bases its criticism of the Church and of the Christian faith on its rejection of the biblical view of the world. Against that it must be urged that the truth and credibility of the biblical message are not dependent on the validity of its view of the world, in which statements built up over about a thousand years are presented at any particular time. The incarnation of God in Christ is involved with the state of knowledge of a definite period of time and a particular cultural situation: the incarnation was an actual event and could not happen otherwise than it did. In the Bible what matters is not the proclamation of a timeless abstract truth, but the testimony to a historical person as the Son of God. The question of the view of the world is of secondary importance.

To take the modern view of the world, which is certainly subject to future modification and so represents nothing final, as the standard and criterion for events and historical figures of the past, is to set it up as an absolute, and to demand of earlier generations something that they could not yet know. The resulting accusations are unfounded and unjust. It is to be expected that in the Bible things and conditions—clothing, housing, social order, food, politics and lots more—should find expression appropriate to the times. Nobody is surprised when Christ asks the pharisee for a denarius, whereas we use other forms of coinage today. Every language and every period has its own images and similies. It is the duty and task of every new generation in its study of the past to uncover the enduring meaning of what was said. Modern speech also uses metaphors and similies which are intelligible, even though later on their original significance is questioned by a process of demythologizing. When we say, for example 'Time wears a red star in its hair', the metaphor is mythological, but the meaning is perfectly clear.

7. *The Contradictions*

In answer to materialistic atheism it must be said that the differences, contradictions and inconsistencies in the Bible to which it calls attention are certainly there, but they are no reason for rejecting its real message. Medieval scholarship discovered such contradictions long ago and found its own explanation of them, so there is nothing at all new in the inconsistencies pointed out by atheism. These inconsistencies would only be confusing, if life could be easily understood rationally. Materialistic atheism is itself aware of the contradictions of existence, not only in nature but also in history, and even attributes to them the capacity to be the driving force of the world. So it is not easy to understand why materialistic atheism objects to the presence of inconsistencies in the Bible, and thinks that in discovering them it has shown the Bible to be unreliable.

This is still more true of the faith witnessed to in the Bible. There are ultimate and insoluble paradoxes in the Bible, more numerous and more profound that a rational superficiality is able to appreciate. 'Many are called but few are chosen' (Matt. 22.14) expresses a profound and insoluble mystery—that faith is the gift of God and yet lack of faith is sin. That does not mean that a man can lay his hands in his lap and leave everything to God. Idleness is no excuse, but is called to account (Matt. 25.14ff). Thus passivity, lethargy and apathy are forbidden to us, as is also activism, i.e. activity for activity's sake. In the light of our knowledge that everything depends on God's mercy and not on our willing or running (Rom. 9.16), and in the light of our faith that the most important thing in life is not taking but accepting (Mark 10.13ff), there is opportunity for action, planning and willing on the part of the Christian. The Holy Scriptures are full of statements testifying to the action of God and describing the new life of the Christian, but they are also full of imperatives which do not leave our actions to our own choice, but make categorical demands upon us. The search for God is imposed upon us whether we will or not, but is also provided with a promise (Jer. 29.13ff). We are further commanded to search the Holy Scriptures (John 5.39). Finally Feuerbach's fear that creation and faith would reduce the world and men to nothing is made nonsense by a single saying of the Apostle Paul: 'We are labourers together with God' (I Cor. 3.9).

The fact that the Bible and faith are beyond complete rational understanding is no argument against them, but simply shows that they are the reflection of a transcendent God. Thus human life and activity receive from above a depth which they could not receive by their own thinking.

What is the Real Conflict between Materialistic Atheism and the Christian Faith?

Materialistic atheism and the Christian faith are conscious of being in ultimate conflict. Materialistic atheism regards itself as possessing all the virtues, and hence builds up a picture of Christianity consisting of errors and faults and so easy to refute. If from all the philosophical, popular scientific and literary writings of materialistic atheism everything that is supposed to be Christianity were put together, the result would be a picture of a Christianity that has never existed. The pattern of the Christian faith is not even approximately correctly described in this extensive literature, but is always distorted. From the Christian standpoint it is difficult to understand why materialistic atheism avoids trying to understand the Christian faith.

1. The Fundamental Conflict

The fundamental conflict between atheism and the Christian faith lies in the fact that atheism interprets the world and man as a self-sufficient entity, and thus as freely organizable, whereas the Christian faith places the reality of God and his revelation in the centre of existence and of human life, and so regards man's destiny as in God's hands.

The conflict between atheism and the Christian faith is not a case of science versus superstition, but of a loosely scientifically based belief in man or in reason or matter versus belief in the triune God. Materialistic atheism rests ultimately on belief in the world and its contents: the Christian faith is based on God the Creator and Ruler of the world. The Christian faith and atheism do not stand opposed as representing faith on the one hand and knowledge on the other, not according to *what* they believe, but ultimately on the object of their belief, *in whom* they believe.

The atheistic belief in purely earthly phenomena takes science into its service, recognizing only those features of science as 'scientific' which in its opinion tend to support atheism or seem likely to be useful to it. On the other hand it separates out as 'unscientific' all those elements of science which seem to threaten atheism or to support belief in God. Nowadays the position of materialistic atheism is such that it no longer dares to base its godlessness on empiricism or logic, but appeals to philosophical-ontological premisses which it has itself discovered. That means that neither experience nor reasoning can lead to a convincing conclusion about the non-existence of God. But a further consequence is that only what materialistic atheism regards as science is recognized in the end as its basis and support.

2. *The View of Man*

All other differences between atheism and the Christian faith derive from this fundamental conflict, particularly with regard to questions about the world and man, nature and history. The question of the view of man cannot and must not be looked at in isolation, but must be considered in relation either to atheism or to belief in God. Nobody saw that so clearly as Feuerbach, and after him Marx and Engels.

Feuerbach regarded man from the biological standpoint, simply as part of nature. Marx retains the theory that man is the highest form of being as the only possible basis for the liberation of Germany, and he demands the emancipation of man and the release of the German from a state of dependency. While Marx started out from his conception of man as the highest form of being, Engels laid more stress on the origin of man in nature: 'The vertebrate in which nature attained its full consciousness is man.' It seems that the liberation of man from dependency and his interpretation solely through nature or society would bring him the desired autonomy and autarchy. But it can be shown that the declaration of the independence of man from God involves him in other dependencies that cannot be set aside.

Feuerbach's main fear, that the creatureliness of man and of nature meant their futility and insignificance, rests on a serious misunderstanding or even a deliberate falsification of the biblical statements about creation. It is not true that the dignity and worth of man and of nature are threatened by their creatureliness. Behind the objection to the creation of man lies hatred of God and hostility to grace. As Marx rightly recognized, it is extremely difficult to make clear to man that he created himself. Man is faced with a momentous choice, whether he is to regard himself as part of nature, the product of matter, the product of society and nothing else, or as God's creature.

The view of man is bound up with the question of the existence of God. Where man regards himself simply as the product of nature and society and denies his relationship to God, then those men who have the power and will are not deterred by 'religion' from treating other men as parts of nature and exploiting them as they wish, for there is then no higher court to call them to account. But where man believes in God, he sees his fellow men as creatures of God like himself and that actually produces a more profound humanity than atheism is able to do.

3. Understanding the World

The understanding of the world is also involved in the question of the existence of God. If this is answered in the atheistic sense and the existence of this world only is accepted, then it follows that our world is eternal in space and time, since firstly no suspicion of any creation must arise, and secondly even the godless man needs something eternal, permanent and secure amid the changes with which he is surrounded. Hence it follows with a certain compelling and inherent logic from the assumption of atheism that the world is without beginning or end, uncreated and hence everlasting. It cannot have any basis or centre or meaning or purpose 'from outside': everything must exist within it. There is a hint here of fear both of the beginning and of the end. The will to self-derived eternity and permanence is supposed to help to overcome these fears.

Engels accepted the permanence of matter and its laws as a 'certainty'. The endlessness of the world in space and time, the 'iron necessity' of the laws of nature, are supposed to provide an inner security that once was found in God. When Engels wrote in 1882, 'Today, however, our conception of the evolution of the universe leaves absolutely no room either for a creator or ruler',[1] he found in the permanence of the universe, matter and its laws the basis for stability and security. But this is bought at the cost of the historicity and reality of nature, its transience and unrepeatability. The decisive factor here is not the insights of the natural sciences, but the changed attitude to life and the changed climate

---

[1] Engels, *Socialism: Utopian and Scientific*, in *The Essential Left* (Marx, Engels, Lenin), London 1960, p. 123.

of opinion. The consciousness of existence is no longer geocentric but cosmic and has been extended into the infinite: only eternity gives meaning and security. What the Christian finds in belief in God is here confined to the world, a world deprived of any 'upward view'. The Christian has a definite sense of eternity: he only asks who represents it.

4. What has Atheism to Offer?

The question of the existence of God is definitive for the view of man and the understanding of the world, but it also affects all other departments of life and culture. Christianity has a right to know what is offered to it by atheism in the way of basic insights and supreme values. What is offered as the foundation and object of faith, love and hope by those who deny God and reject Christ?

The most important answers to this question and the ultimate atheistic criteria make it possible to reach a reliable and responsible conclusion. Marx put forward human self-consciousness as the 'highest divinity' and man as the highest being. Engels refers to the permanence of matter and its laws. Lenin considers the class struggle as the determining force in producing a happy society in the future. Duncker speaks of 'Faith in humanity' and Girnus gives supreme importance to the liberation of the Promethean spirit.

But other philosophers who have contributed to the elaboration of materialistic atheism and are esteemed by it, have made statements about its positive supreme values and ultimate aims. Feuerbach thinks it is not enough to believe in a better life: it must be willed. To that end the love of humanity must replace the love of God as the only true religion, the belief of men in themselves instead of belief in God, the belief that man's fate does not depend on a being outside or above the world, but on man himself. In Bruno Bauer hatred of God is coupled with a boundless confidence in the world. Arthur Drews represents an anti-naturalistic, pantheistic, metaphysically speculative monism, which asserts, as Spinoza did, that God and the world are identical. Although Lenin agrees with Drews in his denial of the historicity of Jesus, he nevertheless criticises his 'shoddy patching up of religion'. Ernst Haeckel, who is highly esteemed by materialistic atheism, formulated his philosophical creed in this way: Above the old outlook of idealism-dualism now falling into ruin rises sublime and glorious the new sun of practical monism revealing the whole temple of nature. In the pure cult of the 'true, good and beautiful' which forms the heart of our new monistic religion we find a rich substitute for the vanished anthropistic ideals 'God, freedom and immortality'.[1]

Challenged by materialistic atheism Christianity is faced with the momentous decision whether to listen to the voice of God in Christ as judgment and salvation or whether to follow material assumptions, values and ideas.

[1] Haeckel, *Die Welträtsel*, Bonn 1903, p. 151f.

7 · Materialistic Atheism and the Existence of God

THE DECISIVE FACT ESTABLISHED BY THE CHRISTIAN faith with reference to materialistic atheism is that it has developed a conception of God which does not in any way correspond with the God revealed in the Bible and witnessed to by Christianity, the Creator of heaven and earth and the Father of our Lord Jesus Christ. It is then a question of momentous importance whether materialistic atheism accepts the testimony of God through Christianity or not. The responsibility of Christianity for the fact that many materialists and atheists have been shocked by Christians and the churches should not be minimized. But the truth of God, his word of judgment and reconciliation to men, is so important that while human shortcomings and misdeeds may well give grounds for criticism, they are not sufficient reason for the rejection of God himself.

Atheism from Feuerbach to the Present Day

Feuerbach had explained God as the product of human imagination. Marx followed him when he wrote in 1843-4: 'As far as Germany is concerned the criticism of religion is in essentials ended. Today theology itself is finished. The only possible practical liberation of Germany is the liberation on the basis of the theory that man is the highest being.'[1] A year later he wrote: 'But since for the socialist the whole of so-called world history is nothing more

[1] Marx-Engels, *On Religion*, pp. 41, 51, 58.

than the development of man through human labour and the development of nature for man, man has incontrovertible evidence of the nature of his origin, his birth by his own efforts. Since the essential nature of man and of nature has become practically observable by the senses, and since man has been recognized as the source of his own existence, the belief in an extraneous being above nature and man, involving the acknowledgment of the non-material quality of nature and man, has become practically impossible. Atheism as a denial of this non-material nature has no longer any meaning, for atheism is a negation of God and by this negation settles the nature of man, but socialism as socialism has no longer any need of this support; it starts out from the theoretically and practically sensuous consciousness of man and of nature as the basis of reality.'[1]

All this means in theory the complete defeat of religion, unconditional denial of God, anthropocentricity and absolute immanence. But Marx was not content with the theoretical refutation of religion, but even aimed at unmasking the Christian cult as immoral and inhuman. On November 30th, 1847, at a meeting of a working men's educational association in London Marx said: 'Among all the achievements of German philosophy the criticism of religion is the most important. All that has been written up till now against the Christian religion has been limited to proving that it was based on false principles . . . but what has not been investigated so far is the practical cult of Christianity. We know that the supreme rite in Christianity is human sacrifice. Now Daumer has demonstrated in a recent book that the Christians really did slaughter human beings and ate human flesh and drank human blood at the Lord's Supper. That explains why the Romans, who tolerated all religions, persecuted the Christians and why later on the Christians destroyed all the heathen literature that was directed against Christianity. Human sacrifice was a sacrament and really existed. Protestantism had only spiritualized it and toned it down. That is why there are more lunatics amongst Protestants than among other sects. By this account set forth in Daumer's book Christianity receives its final blow. What significance can it have for us? It

[1] Marx-Engels, *Kleine ökonomische Schriften*, p. 139.

gives the assurance that the old social system is dying and the edifice of deceit and prejudice is collapsing.'[1]

Thus as far as Marx is concerned the question of the existence of God is solved, religion is refuted, exposed as illusion, and the Christian cult unmasked as inhuman and horrible. Feuerbach had already rejected Daumer's statement about bloody human sacrifices as improbable in 1842, but Marx for a time believed it and used it as a basis of moral refutation of Christianity. Later on (1850) Marx also disowned Daumer's horrible accusation against the Christians and in *Das Kapital* he left Daumer's hypothesis about the Lord's Supper undecided.[2] However he kept to the denial of God and the rejection of Christianity.

Engels believes with Feuerbach that the Christian God is only the imaginative reflection—the mirror image—of man. Engels goes on to say that this God is however the product of a lengthy process of abstraction and is the concentrated quintessence of many tribal and national gods of the past. Similarly man also, whose image this God is, was not an actual man, but likewise the quintessence of many actual men, i.e. the abstract man, and so once again a mental picture.[3]

Lenin thinks that the idea of God, historically and from experience, was compounded of beliefs in spirits, and prejudice taboos derived from ignorance and subjection on the one hand and slavery and monarchy on the other.[4] At the same time Lenin wrote that God was historically and in everyday life mainly a complex of ideas.[5]

Stalin in his famous pamphlet, *Dialectical and Historical Materialism* (1938), saw the position of idealism as regarding the world as the embodiment of the 'absolute idea', the 'world spirit' and 'consciousness', whereas Marx' philosophical materialism started from the theory that the world needed no 'world spirit'.[6]

The assumption that Stalin's expressions 'absolute idea', 'world spirit' and 'consciousness', clearly derived from Hegel, mean,

---

[1] *Marx-Engels Gesamtausgabe*, I 6, p. 639f.

[2] Karl Marx, *Capital*, Everyman Library, 1957, p. 294.

[3] Engels, *Ludwig Feuerbach*, p. 46.   [4] Lenin, *Religion*, pp. 48, 53.

[5] *Op. cit.*, p. 53.

[6] Stalin, *Dialectical and Historical Materialism*, p. 11.

though they do not fit, the God of the Bible is confirmed by numerous statements of modern materialistic authors, who identify Hegel's 'world spirit' with God. Hermann Scheler writes: 'The absolute idea of Hegel is another name for God, that in the same way as the personal God of the Bible story created the world.'[1] *Universe, Earth and Man (Weltall, Erde und Mensch)* goes even further: 'The scientific view as represented by dialectical and historical materialism leaves no place for fairy stories about a "creator", "world spirit" and "ruler".'[2] The biologist Jacob Segal thinks: 'All that happens in the world is nothing but matter and its motion', and 'Primitive man developed the idea of God as a hypothesis to cover up the gaps in his knowledge.'[3]

All the above-mentioned statements about God, and the implication of others, which regard the existence of God as nonsense, and either start from immanent systems of thought or elevate empirical observations into a concept, completely miss the God revealed in the Bible. God is not what the atheistic philosophers think and direct their attacks against, but someone quite different, who is known through his word and accepted by faith, but is not created by philosophy and cannot be refuted by it.

Attempts to find a Philosophical Basis for Materialistic Atheism

Marx and Engels did not confine themselves to assertions, but tried to find a philosophical basis for atheism. Several attempts to do so can be distinguished.

1. The Empirical-Experimental Basis

Materialistic atheism frequently makes use of the general assertion that science has not proved the existence of God. In

---

[1] Scheler, *Die Stellung*, p. 5. Cf. also M. M. Rozental: 'Hegel's absolute idea is a synonym for God, who has been smuggled in, not openly, but in a subtle disguised form' (*Die marxistische dialektische Methode*, Berlin 1953, p. 36). Cf. also more recently Roger Garaudy: 'Hegel's absolute idea is the creator of the world, exactly like God in the Bible. The idea plays the same part in Hegelian philosophy as God does in Christian doctrine' (*Die materialistische Erkenntnistheorie*, Berlin 1960, p. 271). Just as materialistic atheism has tried in recent years to clarify in a general way its relationship to Hegel, so evangelical theology in its turn should try to distinguish clearly its biblical-reformed doctrine from the idealistic-philosophical 'theology of Hegel'.

[2] *Weltall, Erde und Mensch*, 1954, p. 362.

[3] Segal, *Die dialektische Methode in der Biologie*, Berlin 1958, pp. 46, 73, 182.

popular scientific literature statements occur like the one in a report of an aeroplane pilot: 'Stories about God, who is supposed to be enthroned in heaven, strike me as comical. I know what is going on up there, and I have seen no gods there.'[1] Gunter Heyden wrote in an article about the sputniks that man would make still greater discoveries, and never come across a clue that would lead to belief in the existence of any higher being.[2] In reply to both authors it is sufficient to say that invisibility and imperceptibility by the senses is no proof of non-existence. That is true even in everyday experience.

2. *The Historical Basis*

As a defence of atheism it is contended that men have not always believed in God, and so religion is a 'historical category'. The description of the atheistic tradition has already made it clear that in the history of the development of human thought there have almost always been infidels and deniers of God as well as believers. History alone can be the basis neither of belief nor unbelief. The fact that God's revelation in the old covenant and in Christianity took place at definite points of time is no argument against its reality or its binding force.

3. *The Logical Basis*

The philosopher Bela Fogarasi (Budapest) also referred to the proofs of the existence of God in his *Logic* (*Logik*, Berlin 1955), written from the standpoint of dialectical logic and in the spirit of Marx and Engels. He calls the ontological proof arguing in a circle, because it tacitly assumes what is to be proved, and he—like Kant—considers it as refuted.

It is of course true that the ontological proofs of the existence of God put forward by Plato, Aristotle and Archbishop Anselm (1033-1109) are not conclusive, because the idea of a thing is not evidence of its existence. But Fogarasi argues, with Marx, that Kant should have gone further in his refutation of the ontological argument for belief in God. God was only an idea, the product

---

[1] Pavyolkin, *Der religiöse Aberglaube*, p. 165.
[2] *Neues Deutschland*, 4/12/1957.

of imagination, 'and so this proof is nothing more than the proof of the non-existence of God'.[1] Fogarasi's conclusion is illogical. If hypotheses and proofs dating from earlier centuries are no longer valid in view of the advance of modern science, this is only a reflection on the position of earlier ontology and logic, and not on the object to be proved. In other words, the collapse of the proofs of the existence of God, particularly at the hands of the idealist Kant, only means that God refuses to allow himself to be imprisoned within the limits of human logic: he cannot be either proved or disproved logically. Fogarasi had to admit this when he contradicted himself two pages later and like Spinoza said: 'Ignorance is no argument. The fact that we do not know a thing does not mean that it does not exist, nor that its existence is not provable. Ignorance proves nothing.' Thus the fact that God cannot be proved, but insists on being believed, proves nothing against his existence.

4. The Ontological Basis

By this is understood the attempt to prove the non-existence of God with the help of an ontology, a definite materialistic doctrine of being. Such ontological statements cannot be derived from formal logic alone, which deals only with the processes of thought and so cannot make pronouncements on the nature of being, but derive their material mainly, whether they admit it or not, from experience and the observation of the material world.

One ontological principle of materialistic atheism states: 'The world is by nature material.' In the relevant literature this leads to atheistic consequences in this way: If in our investigation of the world we never encounter anything immaterial, then the world is just material. But if the world is just material then it is knowable through the senses. From that a conclusion of wide significance is drawn, that only matter (perhaps also its motion and laws) exists and nothing else. Everything that exists is a purely this-wordly phenomenon and is ultimately of material origin. This statement does not of course deny the existence of immaterial, spiritual and psychological phenomena, but these are regarded

---

[1] Fogarasi, *Logik*, p. 347.

only in relation to and as products of matter. From this premiss materialistic atheism comes to the conclusion that the structure of this world consists in its material nature and so logically excludes the existence of God.

Another ontological thesis of materialistic atheism says: 'The world is knowable.' This statement is within limits true and is evidence of a practical and theoretical epistemological optimism. It acquires its atheistic implication by its interpretation in the sense that what is not knowable (via the senses) does not exist. Knowability means the possibility of formulating laws. But where laws are known, formulated and tested by practice (which is recognized as the most important criterion of truth) there is, according to atheistic logic, no room left for religion, in the sense of the predominantly rational understanding of religion by materialistic atheism. In this sense Lenin says: 'The expulsion of laws from science is in reality only a way of smuggling in the laws of religion.'[1] This is the root of materialistic atheism's dislike of agnosticism, positivism, relativism, subjectivism, etc. For all these would leave over unknowable fragments, and that means a back door for the invasion of idealism and religion. On the other hand materialistic atheism believes that where science has known and tested laws, the possibilty of the existence of religion is destroyed, because in its opinion religion only survives on the unknown. In other words knowledge and science inhibit religion and faith. Thus the thesis that the world is knowable is transformed into another thesis: 'Only what is knowable or known exists.' This extension of the original thesis is supposed to furnish a proof of the truth of atheism.

A third ontological thesis of materialistic atheism says: 'Being, nature and matter are primary; consciousness, thought and mind are secondary.' This thesis is at first admissible, but it becomes false when the secondary entities—consciousness, thought and mind—are identified with God, and then the conclusion is drawn that matter produces thought and mind and these in turn produce the idea of God. This would only be true under Feuerbach's assumption, which is contestable, and under the assumptions of

[1] Rozental, *Die marxistische dialektische Methode*, p. 74.

other idealistic and materialistic philosophers, who regard God
as the product of the human brain. But this contradicts the testimony of the Christian faith and does not fit the God that it confesses. All the three ontological theses of materialistic atheism may
remain philosophically undecided, but what the Bible testifies to
about God and what Christianity confesses is untouched by them.

Georg Klaus indicated another attempt to find a basis for
atheism, likewise derived from materialistic ontology. He maintains that the existing insights of dialectical materialism makes the
acceptance of the existence of God superfluous. Among these
insights are the doctrines of 'universal reciprocal action' and the
'self-movement of things'. Causality, the law of cause and effect,
is only one element in the universal reciprocal action[1] and is not
sufficient explanation of the relationships of reality.[2] Indeed the
three conditions under which causality occurs purely and exactly
are strictly speaking nowhere realized.[3]

It is characteristic of the situation of materialistic atheism of
most recent date that it has relaxed the insistence on the principle
of mechanical materialism, that everything has its cause and every
movement its stimulus, and concentrated on internal causes.
'Actually things and phenomena are not in the first place produced
by external causes, but by internal causes.'[4] These internal causes
are crucial. Klaus rejects the idea that a chain of causes and effects
must necessarily have an initial impulse. So Klaus built a bridge
between logic and ontology, between philosophy and cosmology,
between thought and the universe. He draws also extremely
important conclusions: 'The law of universal reciprocal action and
the fact of the inner contradictions of things would make superfluous a creator of the world and a first cause that is itself without
cause. The world is self-sufficient. What the Thomists predicated
of God is true of the world. That does not mean that some finite
phenomenon in the universe is exclusively determined by the
internal conditions of its system. It is only true of the universe as
a whole.'[5]

---

[1] Klaus, *Jesuiten, Gott, Materie*, Berlin 1957, p. 307.
[2] *Op. cit.*, p. 313.   [3] *Op. cit.*, p. 316.   [4] *Op. cit.*, p. 317.
[5] *Op. cit.*, p. 318.

Thus Georg Klaus states that the world as a whole is self-sufficient, is its own cause and revolves by itself. This ontological climate and the statements that definite insights of dialectical materialism would make the existence of God superfluous are not a philosophical perception or the result of scientific investigation, but are ideological-atheistic presuppositions that cannot be proved.

A fifth point of view bearing on the ontological basis of atheism and entering into the scientific-cosmological field has been put forward by Olof Klohr. He says in fact that subjection to natural laws is universal, but then goes on to say that the causal relationship must not be transferred to the world as a whole by assuming a non-provable divinity as the cause of this world.[1]

When Georg Klaus tries to settle the question of the cause and origin of this world by reference to its self-sufficiency, and when Klohr tries to settle it by forbidding the use of causality to the world as a whole, the atheistic motives behind their statements becomes transparently clear, i.e. that under no circumstances must any creation of the world be allowed to enter the field of vision. For then immediately the question of a creator would arise and the whole edifice of materialistic atheism would be endangered. Klohr openly and clearly avoids this consequence when he says: 'From the standpoint of science and of dialectical materialism the question of the origin of the world is meaningless, because the world is eternal.'[2]

Quite recently an afterthought about the basis of atheism has been put forward from the materialistic-atheistic side: The eternity of the world, which would exclude any creation and any creator, cannot indeed be demonstrated by empirical research, since this can only deal with finite things and phenomena, but empirical research is not the only scientific activity: 'Empirical research is however not enough in itself for the complete discovery of truth. Philosophical thinking must be added to it.'[3] This interesting admission means that the idea of the eternity of the

[1] Klohr, *Naturwissenschaft, Religion und Kirche*, Berlin 1958, p. 48.
[2] *Op. cit.*, p. 49.
[3] R. Kirchhoff, *Wissenschaftliche Weltanschauung, und religiöser Glaube*, Berlin 1958, p. 50.

world cannot be based on empirical research alone, but is the result of philosophical thinking of atheistic origin. As neither formal logic nor empirical research can pronounce upon the existence or non-existence of God, there is only 'philosophical thinking' left, i.e. atheistic ontology as the source of atheism, and that is a field beyond logic and empiricism. In the end these considerations lead not to scientifically demonstrable facts of generally valid nature, but only to the root of atheistic ideology, which means faith-judgment and wish-fulfilment, which cannot be logically convincing or evident through induction or deduction.

We are left with the conviction that the scientific outlook of materialistic atheism comes from the prior assumption of the non-existence of God, and thus from definite self-postulated premisses and not from any scientifically assured evidence. Within this limitation any scientific research inevitably leads to the same result from which it started out.

Attempts at a Scientific Basis for Materialistic Atheism

Materialistic atheism denies God and therefore denies a creation. The question is, On whom does the onus of proof lie? Fogarasi asserts emphatically the principle derived from Roman law: 'The onus of proof lies with the one who affirms and not with him who denies.'[1] Now materialistic atheism is not content with denying the existence of God and rejecting creation, but feels compelled to shoulder the burden of proving that the world is eternal in space and time, without beginning or end, uncreated and imperishable. This obligation gives force to the arguments and investigations, which would otherwise be difficult to understand. The fundamental question 'Where did the world come from?' raises other closely related questions: 'Where did the solar system come from?' 'Whence came life?' 'Whence came man?' To all these questions materialistic atheism tries to find a philosophical answer in accordance with its own presuppositions and seeks to support it with empirically reliable material. It starts out from definite methodological and ontological presuppositions, which are accepted without testing, and then reaches results in accordance with its own

[1] Fogarasi, *Logik*, p. 349.

solution. An analysis of the principles of philosophical dialectics
and philosophical materialism with reference to their presuppositions and aims, under the general theme 'Creation or the eternity
of the world' would throw quite a new light on our question and
show that the atheistic background has powerfully influenced the
philosophic foundation.

1. Attempt at a Cosmological Basis

In order to show the close connection between the rejection of
creation and the assertion of the eternity of matter we may quote
from *Deutsche Zeitschrift für Philosophie* the contention of an
atheistic materialist that a world finite in time is inconsistent with
the materialistic answer to the fundamental question, since the
presence of non-eternal matter would at once raise the question
of its creator. 'But in fact this materialistic answer to the fundamental question is confirmed by all human experience; hence
dialectical materialism maintains as the consequence of the solution
of the fundamental question everywhere confirmed, that the world
is eternal and permanent, and this is in complete agreement with
natural science, which, unfortunately for idealism, finds no
evidence anywhere of a world finite in space and time.'[1]

Pfaffe and Neumann in their pamphlet *No Room for God in the
Universe* (*Kein Platz für Gott im Weltall*, Berlin 1958) wrote:
'Dialectical materialism maintains that the world is eternal in
space and time. Matter had no beginning nor will it one day have
an end. Besides the most diverse forms of self-moving matter
existing in time and space there is nothing, and certainly not a
nothing from which anything began spontaneously or might be
created by a divine spirit.'[2]

Since Stalin said that the world needed no 'world spirit'
numerous variations on this theme have appeared. Subbotin
writes: 'The idea of the creation of the world out of nothing has no
intelligible meaning.'[3] Voronzov-Velyaminov carried this idea
further: 'The universe is infinite in space and time. It has always

---

[1] *Deutsche Zeitschrift für Philosophie*, 1958/1/144.
[2] Pfaffe-Neumann, *Kein Platz*, p. 42.
[3] Subbotin, *So wurde die Erde*, Vienna 1947, p. 11; Subbotin, *Entstehung
und Alter der Erde*, Berlin 1953, p. 3.

existed and will always exist.'[1] Suvorov expanded this subjec-
tively: 'There are no limits to man's capacity for knowledge.'[2]

Guryev wrote similarly: 'The universe is in everlasting motion
and it is certain that no gods are needed to set it and keep it in
motion. There is no room or function for gods in the universe.'[3]
Sytinskaya commends Gordiano Bruno for his insistence on the
eternity of the universe.[4] Fedynski states that the universe is
infinite.[5] Shevlyakov asks: 'Did the world have a beginning and
will it have an end?' and answers: 'The Soviet astronomers
maintain that the whole universe or matter is eternal. The universe
had no beginning, neither will it have an end. Within it matter is
in eternal circulation, assuming various forms and shapes, and no
divine supernatural powers have ever interfered in the natural
course of this evolution.'[6] Guryev says in another place: 'The
world is material, eternal in time and infinite in space. It changes
and develops according to its own internal law. No part of it is
derived from nothing.' 'Matter is not only the natural source of
our sensations, but also the prime cause of all processes of nature.'
In this connection Guryev gives an important hint of his interpretation of the world: 'The world must be understood from within
itself, from the properties of matter. That is one of the most
important materialistic principles, on which real progressive
science rests, and by which it is fundamentally distinguished from
every religion.' The followers of religion and the idealists recognize
the creation of the world as fundamental and so deny the eternity
of matter. The materialists, in agreement with the findings of
science and experience, affirm the eternity of matter, 'and so
exclude every idea of the creation of the world and of anything
supernatural, and find the cause of all phenomena in the motion
of matter. Thus we have to do with two irreconcilable views of the
world, the religious-idealistic view and the scientific-atheistic.'[7]

[1] Voronzov-Velyaminov, *Der Aufbau des Weltalls*, Berlin 1952, p. 24.

[2] Suvorov, *Was uns der Lichtstrahl erzählt*, Berlin 1954, p. 68.

[3] Guryev, *Was ist das Weltall?*, Vienna 1947, p. 15.

[4] Sytinskaya, *Gibt es Leben auf anderen Planeten?*, Berlin 1954, p. 4.

[5] Fedynski, *Himmelsteine, Meteorite und Meteore*, Berlin 1952, p. 22.

[6] Shevlyakov, *Gab es einen Anfang der Welt und wird es ein Ende geben?*,
Berlin 1954, p. 26.

[7] Guryev, *Wissenschaftliche Voraussicht*, Berlin 1958, p. 6f.

Rudolf Rochhausen writes: 'Within the framework of the universe there is neither beginning nor end, neither new creation nor destruction of matter, but only an eternal transformation.' 'Matter needs therefore no spiritual power, no divine will; instead it develops according to objectively existing laws.'[1] Against Pope Pius XII Rochhausen writes: 'The Soviet scientists oppose to the unscientific Christian idea of a finite world the view of dialectical materialism, which recognizes the cosmos as infinite in time and space. This interpretation forms the basis and the programme of its cosmological and cosmogonic theories.'[2]

Herbert Gute writes: 'Dialectical materialism maintains that the world is material, eternal in time and infinite in space, that it changes and develops according to its own internal laws, that no part of it is derived from nothing, that the wide variety of natural and social phenomena is nothing but the endless evolution of matter, its transformation from one form of existence to another.'[3] In similar vein Werner Schuffenhauer says that Feuerbach opposed to the theory of the creation of the world from nothing 'the materialistic conception of the eternity and inexhaustibility of matter, and the concept of space and time as objective forms of matter'.[4] Olof Klohr writes: 'All available evidence points to the infinity of the universe.' He goes on to defend himself against any suggestion of 'faith': 'Dialectical materialism maintains that the world is eternal, that no God created it, but that it has always existed. This assertion is not just an article of belief of dialectical materialism, as unproven as the religious belief in the creation of the world.'[5]

Walter Hollitscher joins the ranks of those who regard the question of the creation of the world as meaningless: 'The natural history of the universe has of course no "beginning", indeed it is complete nonsense to inquire about the beginning of the universe.' 'The world was not knocked together in space and time. There are no limits set to man's urge for investigation, for the universe

---

[1] Rochhausen, *Der Sputnik und der liebe Gott*, Berlin 1958, p. 11f.
[2] *Op. cit.*, p. 22f.   [3] Gute, *Glauben oder Wissen*, 1958, p. 12f.
[4] Schuffenhauer, *Der Mensch schuf Gott*, Berlin 1958, p. 13.
[5] Klohr, *Naturwissenschaft*, pp. 57 and 59.

itself is boundless. It was not created and will never perish: it has neither beginning nor end.'[1]

All these many voices however are actually singing the same tune—the passionate rejection of creation and the equally passionate conviction of the eternity of the world and of matter.

There is one more voice to be heard in this connection—Rolf Kirchhoff: 'Dialectical materialism draws from the empirically proven law of the constancy and transformation of mass and energy the scientific conclusion that matter is uncreatable and indestructible and that it is an endless process.' 'The eternity of matter is proved by the results of science. It is quite inconsistent with any form of belief in God. It expresses the consequent scientific-atheistic character of dialectical materialism.'[2]

One other quotation goes even further than Kirchhoff in attempting to refute the 'Christ legend' by means of the principle of the eternity of the world: 'Science has long since refuted the idea of the creation of the world. It has established that the universe has no beginning and no end, no form and no centre, and extends infinitely in every direction. With this fact the legend which is at the heart of Christian doctrine, that Christ the mythical Son of God, delivered men from their sins, loses its justification.'[3]

It can be seen from these quotations that for materialistic atheism the question of the existence of God finds its focus in the question of the eternity of the world, as Engels had indicated. There are supporters of materialistic atheism who in spite of the advances in the natural sciences still hold to the old position of monistic materialism as it was at the turn of the century. Hermann Ley said in 1955 and wrote in 1957: 'Dialectical materialism should appropriate from the past the most important intellectual arguments that have proved to be crucial in the conflict between materialism and idealism, namely the doctrine of the eternity of matter, the concept of man as a part of nature, the doctrine that the world can be explained, the rejection of superstition and miracle through the recognition of an absolute conformity to natural laws, which

---

[1] Hollitscher, *Die Entwicklung im Universum*, Berlin 1951, p. 15f.
[2] Kirchhoff, *Wissenschaftliche Weltanschauung*, p. 51.
[3] W. A. Mesenzev and L. A. Druyanov, *Kann man die Zukunft voraussehen?*, Berlin 1959, p. 51.

includes unconditional causality.' Ley adds to this list 'These
theories are completely opposed to any belief in a creation or an end
to the world. They disprove the existence of any spiritual principle
outside the coherence of nature and deny the immortality of the
so-called soul.'[1]

2. *The Biological Basis*

Neither philosophical nor scientific knowledge has any independent function within the framework of materialistic-atheistic
ideology, but instead both are made to serve the atheistic involvement in the fundamental question. That does not prevent useful
results from being achieved in particular details not directly
bearing on atheism, but in areas which overlap into the philo-
sophical-ideological field definite tendencies prejudice the investigation and its methods and content.

That is true also in the biological field and its problems. Here the
important question is, What is life ? and then the investigation of its
'natural' origin. In this connection sensational results have been
published by A. I. Oparin[2] and previously also by O. B. Lepeshchinskaya.[3] However, attempts at the synthetic production of life
become tangled up here in the atheistic motives, so that theoretical
scientific progress and the hoped-for artificial production of life
are supposed to refute the original creation of the first life on earth.
These atheistic conclusions, however, do not stand up to examination, for if the artificial production of life does not occur spontaneously, but only through human agency, then the origin of life
still remains unexplained.

The second biological problem is the origin of species in the
sense of Michurin's development of Darwinism.[4] The question
here is not concerned with the legitimate influence of man on
fauna and flora in the interests of the consumer, but with a natural,
i.e. atheistic, explanation of the existing conditions in the realm of
animals and plants. The narrow limits of the possibility of human

[1] Ley, *Friedrich Engels philosophische Leistung*, p. 22.
[2] A. I. Oparin, *Die Entstehung des Lebens*, Berlin/Leipzig 1949 and Berlin
1957.
[3] O. B. Lepeshchinskaya, *Die Entstehung von Zellen aus lebender Materie*,
Berlin 1952.
[4] I. W. Michurin, *Ausgewählte Schriften*, Berlin 1953; 2nd ed. 1957.

influence and the very long period of time necessary for 'natural' evolution are admitted, but the last word is not yet spoken about the force and direction of the actual evolution of individual species.

The third problem in the biological field is the question of teleology. Engels believed that Darwin had given the *coup de grâce* to teleology, which postulated a purposive creator. 'Teleology is a "sport" of idealism and a very important constituent of every religious view of the world.'[1]

Recently there has been less inclination than formerly to deny purpose and meaning in the biological field. That is apparent in Lysenko's *Law of Life of Biological Species* (*Lebensgesetz der biologischen Arten*). The first version of this law (*Pravda*, 17/7/1957) said: 'In animals, plants and micro-organisms in free nature the different organs, features, physiological processes, and the whole infinite complexity of peculiarities, forms and functions of the organism have the object directly or indirectly of promoting the numerical increase of the species, even when in some individual cases this shortens their lives or leads to their death. On the basis of this law of biological species, supported by the laws of heredity and variation set forth in Michurin's genetics and backed by practical experiment, it is possible to solve many questions that are important both for the practice and for the further development of biology.'[2] The second and later version of the law of biological species (*Isvestia*, 8/12/1957) states that the life processes are directed towards a quantitative increase of life, not of course of life in general, but an increase of life of the species concerned. In the case of a normal and not pathological living organism therefore its whole construction and condition, all its qualities and processes, the whole complexity of its claims on living conditions, and also the complex reactions to the influence of the external environment necessary for this organism, all this is in one way or another directed so that the actual biological species concerned should increase numerically. This remains true even if in the process the life of a particular individual is shortened or even its natural death is brought about.[3]

[1] J. T. Frolov, *Darwinismus und Teleologie*, Leipzig/Jena 1958, p. 12.
[2] *Soviet Union Press*, 1957/88/1915 (4/8/57).
[3] *Soviet Union Press*, 1958/10/191 (24/1/58).

3. The Anthropological Basis

Anthropology defined as the science of physical nature and the origin of man has an indirect function in materialistic atheism. It has to show both the relationship between man and the animal world and also to explain all the features which in the progress of evolution characterize man as qualitatively distinct from the animals.[1]

The theory of the origin of species is particularly popular with atheism in order to prove the truth of atheism by anthropogony. Thus it is maintained that Linnaeus destroyed the biblical legend of the creation of man by God, and that Darwin had proved that man was not created by God, but is the highest stage in the evolutionary process.[2]

Has the Question of the Existence of God really been solved by Materialistic Atheism?

Materialistic atheism asserts flatly and in general terms that atheism is godlessness based on scientific knowledge or that is a scientifically based denial of religion, belief in miracles and in a future life.[3]

The opinions of some individual scientists about the supposed philosophical and scientific basis of atheism have already been briefly indicated. It remains to be investigated whether the question of the existence of God has really been settled.

1. The Collapse of the 'Proofs' of the Existence of God has led to a New Understanding of Faith

The more serious atheistic literature refers now and then to the refutation of the 'proofs' of the existence of God, and draws from that the conclusion that atheism is right. This conclusion is unwarranted, for, looked at from a philosophical angle, it is clear that faith cannot prove the existence of God, but neither can atheism disprove it. The Church cannot produce any proof of God to atheism either of materialistic or idealistic kind. The earlier attempts to prove the existence of God failed. They were

[1] *Anthropologie* (GSE), Jena 1954, p. 3.
[2] *Mensch, woher, wohin?*, pp. 31 and 39.
[3] *Volksfremdwörterbuch*, Berlin 1953; *Lexikon A-Z*.

considered valid for centuries, because the existence of God was neither doubted nor denied, but they were unable to stand up to critical philosophical examination. It was Kant in the first place who refuted the 'proofs' of the existence of God so convincingly that they have since then been of only historical interest.

But the existence and the revelation of God were not affected in any way by the breakdown of the 'proofs'. It is true even in secular matters that the inadequacy of a proof is not evidence against the existence and reality of the object to be proved, but only indicates that the object is not intellectually as comprehensible, logically convincing or empirically demonstrable as had been previously assumed. The breakdown of the 'proofs', in spite of the surprise and painful shock that it caused, produced in the end a very salutary and important understanding of faith, namely the insight that God cannot be grasped from below, like touching or feeling with hands, as is the case with other earthly-human objects. Neither can God be compressed into the human laws of logic. God is the transcendent Lord and Creator, who cannot be found just where a man thinks he should be found, but chooses to be sought and found where he pleases. With the breakdown of the 'proofs' a new light has come to the Church and to Christianity, namely the realization that they cannot base the reason, task and aim of their work in the world either on philosophy or history, either on society or science, but only on its unique foundation, the Holy Scriptures, the word of God, the person of Jesus Christ.

Basically the crucial point had already been appreciated and stated by Luther. But in the following centuries the Church and theology has again and again 'enriched' itself with all sorts of buttresses and supports from apparently allied cultural fields. Thus a process began that has lasted a whole century, a process of austerity and rigour, till at last the Church realized that 'German idealism' was not its ally, but a dangerous enemy. The Church and Christianity have had to learn to think seriously about the basis of their faith: the figure of Jesus Christ and his word. Only so have they been able to defeat the attacks associated with such names as Feuerbach, Nietzsche, Haeckel and Rassenwahn, and have issued purified from the conflict.

The Church has realized that, where the voice of God in the Gospel is heard, man ceases to be an irresponsible, self-centred being, and thenceforth faces decisions of the greatest responsibility. The new atheistic propaganda suffers essentially from the fact that it has not yet shown any awareness at all of this fundamental new orientation of the evangelical faith, but is still fighting against an image of Christianity such as hardly existed even in the past. The limitations of atheistic propaganda are quite obvious today, for it never even touches the real question of the reality of God, because this question lies beyond all propaganda. Popular scientific literature particularly misses the heart of the problem completely, takes refuge in distortion, draws unwarranted conclusions, and makes reference to single statements by authors who wrote fifty to a hundred years ago and who could not possibly foresee the latest developments either of the sciences or theology.

2. Have the Natural Sciences defeated Atheistic Ontology?

Feuerbach and Marx made no secret of their atheistic attitude and confessed it openly. For both of them the question of God was solved in so far as they denied the existence of God and so only needed to trace back the phenomenon of religion and the idea of God to their human earthly origin. Feuerbach undertook this task with such passion and erudition that Marx and Engels at once became 'Feuerbachians', accepted his refutation as convincing, and as far as a negative answer to the question of God is concerned, remained lifelong adherents of Feuerbach, so that Feuerbach's work still continues to exercise a powerful influence.

But in all this there is still one question that remains to be answered. If, as is alleged, God does not exist, where did the world come from? What about the creation? Feuerbach and Marx were doubtless aware that this question was still unanswered, and so strove with all their intellectual power to solve it in an atheistic sense. Both misinterpreted the idea of creation and deduced from it without warrant the unreality of the world, the futility of man, the non-necessity of nature and the dependence of existence. The idea of having to live by the favour of someone else was intolerable to Marx, just as he considered subservience the worst of crimes, and wanted to see the self-reliant Prometheus honoured as a saint and martyr. Thus his will and intellect struggled through to a self-existent nature and man, even in the face of the clear evidence of practical experience. He did not want to be the creature of God, but his own creature.

The seriousness and depth of such a deliberate intellectual passion becomes clear against the biblical background. The Apostle Paul says: By the grace of God I am what I am. In the same way the atheistic standpoint might be expressed: By my own work and my own thinking I am, as a human being, the product of myself. An atheism of such depth is rare in western thought. It appears perhaps in the *Prometheus* poem of young Goethe, then in the subjective idealism of Fichte, and finally in Nietzsche, who wrote in *Zarathustra*: 'If there were any gods, how could I endure not to be a god ? So there are no gods! I drew the conclusion: now it draws me.'

Materialistic atheism supports this ontological, ideological self-sufficiency primarily by the scientific theory of the permanence and eternity of the world. But it is open to question whether this scientifically assured autonomous view of existence held by materialistic atheism can be made tenable and intelligible in the face of modern science. Is the monistic-immanent ontology as it was formulated as a 'new creed' about 1900 and put into the mouth of a sixth-former of 1892 still possible today ? Theophilus—that was the name of the sixth-former—enunciated his new creed in this way: 'The universe is eternal and infinite. It is sustained by two supreme laws, the conservation of matter and the conservation of energy. Everything has its origin in the combination of elements, of which there are a definite number. They are modifications of a primary element, that will be discovered in the distant future, when the dreams of the alchemists of the transformation of elements will be fulfilled. The smallest unit of matter is the atom— spherical, rigid, indivisible and unchangeable. The cosmos in its unified structure and in its uninterrupted motion consists of an infinite number of these atoms. Every minute it kindles new suns in different parts of empty space and extinguishes others for a long, perhaps eternal night.'[1]

[1] Parandovski, *Himmel in Flammen*, Berlin 1957, p. 293.

In this sense Viktor Stern advocated the thesis of absolute space and absolute time,[1] but it was pointed out (in 1957) by the editorial board of the *Deutsche Zeitschrift für Philosophie* that his theory of absolute space was in contradiction to the modern theory of relativity, so further discussion has little point.[2] Robert Havemann, who had previously supported the materialistic-atheistic position in *Universe, Earth and Man*, was criticised in 1957 because the principles of materialistic-atheistic ideology that he maintained, e.g. the eternity of the world, had been attacked and abandoned, because they could not be proved experimentally and so were dogmatic-theological statements (*sic*).[3]

But there are other voices that are important in this connection. Paul Ahnert writing in 1957 on the question whether the universe was infinite said that the present state of knowledge weighs the balance slightly in favour of a finite universe. Nothing is yet decided: the road to a solution must be by observation, not by speculation, feeling or prejudice.[4] Arnold Zweig in an article on Einstein in the book *Our Germany* distributed at the Youth Festival in 1957, wrote that the substance of the theory of relativity was that the universe was no longer regarded as an infinite system, time was no longer considered absolute, light was subject to gravity, and all quantities of time and space were dependent on the movement of the observer at the time.[5]

Still more important in this connection are the following voices from the year 1958. Pfaffe and Neumann attempted to find a balance between the ontological statement of the infinity of the world in space and time and the scientific evidence of the finiteness of the world, with the help of the dialectical concept of the unity, and the conflict of opposites and with the help of the 'general contraction' of dialectical logic. In this way they tried to retain the old without excluding the new. They maintained that one of the many contradictions and the most general in the universe consists in the fact that the whole universe is infinite, but all its

[1] *Wissenschaftliche Annalen,* 1957/6/410.
[2] *Deutsche Zeitschrift für Philosophie,* 1957/1/114.
[3] *Neues Deutschland,* 29/1/57.
[4] *Kalendar für Sternfreunde,* Leipzig 1957, p. 147.
[5] *Unser Deutschland,* p. 354f.

parts, in which it is expressed, are finite in space and time.[1] Neither logically nor empirically do Pfaffe and Neumann make clear how an infinite whole can result from a number of finite parts. This criticism also applies to the statement of Kurt Hager that science really demonstrates 'that the infinite is formed out of the finite, from finite transient things, but is nevertheless infinite'.[2]

3. Has the Existence of God been Finally Disproved?

As we have seen, the attempt is made to accept the evidence of the finiteness of the world supplied by science, by referring to finite parts and transient things, and at the same time clinging to the infinity of the whole. This is an unresolved situation. How can parts which are finite in time and space produce a total infinite universe? This is to succumb to speculation and to postulate something that is neither observable nor logically necessary. Such assumptions are obviously derived from ontological-atheistic premisses which hitherto have insisted on an infinite world. The idea of a creation must on no account be allowed to arise.

When these changes of attitude on the part of competent spokesmen are viewed against the background of the monistic-materialistic ontology of the end of last century, the attempt by modern materialistic atheism to bring itself into harmony with the assured results of modern science is noteworthy. It is not that the recognition of the finitude of our universe might lead to the immediate conclusion that there was creation after all, or that it might be said that science is moving towards religion, but it does mean that barriers and prejudices against faith that were set up over sixty years ago, not by science but by a monistic-materialistic ontology built on it, turn out to be an ideological rather than a purely scientific reservation against belief in God as the creator and the world as the work of his hands. The barriers have now been largely broken down by science itself and the road is clear for serious research scientists to pursue science with complete intellectual honesty, while retaining their belief in God. And the Church in its turn is free to abandon its former inflexible attitude

---

[1] Pfaffe-Neumann, *Kein Platz*, p. 48.
[2] Hager, *Der dialektische Materialismus*, Berlin 1958, p. 82.

to scientific investigation and to forsake its over-precipitate and
often erroneous conclusions. The conclusions drawn by Feuerbach
and others that belief in a creator meant that the world as creation
is futile and that man as the creature of God is worthless have
turned out to be erroneous interpretations of belief in creation.
The right road leads along the middle way between the extremes
of world idolatry and world contempt.

To take this world seriously, to recognize our task in it, and to
find a good and meaningful way of life, does not depend on believ-
ing that the world is eternal and infinite. The eternity and infinity
of the world and the estimated time of the existence of man on it
as some 100,000 years do not offer any solution of the inevitability
of death or the problem of guilt. Death and guilt must in the end
be overcome individually with personal responsibility and often in
deepest loneliness.

Some of the ideas of materialistic atheism are not really so far
from the witness of the Bible to the end of the world as popular
scientific literature sometimes makes out. Engels envisages with
sober realism a point in time when the animals with the capacity
to reason, having discovered viable conditions, are mercilessly
destroyed.[1]

One motive for materialistic atheism to resist the idea of a
beginning of the world is the fear of having to accept as a consequence an end to the world, for it believes that this consequence
would impede the energy and confidence in life, and so play into
the hands of its political and ideological opponents. But is it
possible to form an accurate judgment on the basis of a prejudice,
or to refute the idea of a beginning with the fear of the end? The
fact that every individual human life had a beginning which we
celebrate annually, and that the human race had a beginning,
although there is much conflict about the cause and time and place,
which it may be impossible ever to clear up completely, and
the fact that there was a beginning to the lowest forms of organic
life—these facts are not only not denied by materialistic atheism,
but are accepted and investigated. Why should the logically
convincing and obvious conclusion of a corresponding end be

[1] Engels, *Dialectics of Nature*, Moscow 1954, p. 54.

regarded as a complete fabrication? To face this end without falling into defeatism or nihilism is a task laid upon us by everyday observation and by the structure of this life, and is not a bogey-man invented by idealists or the adherents of religion.

Life has a beginning in history, which materialistic atheism admits by its passionate investigation of it. Man has not always existed, as materialistic atheism admits, but at some time 'originated' (When? Where? How? Why?). So too this earth of ours, the planetary system and the solar systems, the exact number of which we do not know.

The natural sciences, which at the turn of the century seemed to be a stronghold of materialistic atheism, have been so transformed since then that they tend to support rather than oppose a genuine belief in God. The materialistic philosopher Bela Fogarasi admitted this, although reluctantly, when he wrote in 1953: 'In the annual conferences of the Association of German Scientists and Doctors we used to hear materialistic or almost materialistic lectures from men like Helmholz, Hertz, Nernst and Planck. At the conference in 1951 the physicist Kienle stated that the nature of thought cannot be understood on the basis of the natural sciences, from which it follows that it is a matter for the philosophers and theologians.'[1]

Christians can only regard these changes with caution, and must not immediately assume conclusions beyond the intention of the authors, but they may well take up with the greatest sympathy the unsettled problems and re-examine past errors, bearing in mind their own blameworthy involvement, and share to the best of their ability in the task of restatement for the future.

The philosophical-ontological part of materialistic atheism is not so firmly established, and thanks to the principle of dialectics not so rigid, that it could not give up the motives that give a negative answer to the question of the existence of God. The crucial factor here will be whether the consequences drawn from the theory of materiality and knowability are fully sustained or not. These theses are not empirically provable and so the consequences are not logically convincing. In the philosophic

[1] Fogarasi, *Kritik des physikalischen Idealismus*, Berlin 1953, p. 111f.

structure of materialistic atheism there are starting points which the atheistic premisses and consequences show to be not essential. With some reserve attention may now be drawn to these.

Science has set objective limitations to existence which must not be overlooked by philosophy. The Planck quantum of action and Einstein's formula $E=mc^2$ and also Heisenberg's uncertainty principle represent such limitations. Prudent materialistic-atheistic authors admit such limitations to knowledge and existence and avoid the popular scientific fantasy of absolute knowability. The materialistic philosopher Viktor Stern, who was inclined on materialistic grounds to assert the absolutism and objectivity of time and space, denied the unlimited possibility of knowing. He says for example: 'We shall never completely know it (the universe). Our knowledge is a picture of reality but is never complete. It is always only a part of inexhaustible reality. We shall also never completely understand objective space and time.'[1] It would be a naïve illusion 'that we could ever be in a position to state completely of any movement how it was produced, i.e. to find an absolute system of relationship. That would be equivalent to a complete understanding of the infinite',[2] which Stern obviously does not claim. He rightly asserts that it is error and nonsense to adhere to the view that 'only that exists which is observed or observable.' 'There are an infinite number of things that we are unaware of, do not observe and cannot measure, but which nevertheless exist.'[3] Bela Fogarasi expresses much the same view in other words. Referring to Spinoza's principle that ignorance is no argument Fogarasi rightly says: 'It does not follow from the fact that we do not know something that it does not exist or that its existence cannot be proved.'[4]

These limitations to knowledge, which are admitted by the more prudent materialistic philosophers, are of fundamental importance and practical consequence in three ways.

Firstly in connection with the knowledge of the past and of distant space. Any realist must recognize, without falling into agnosticism or scepticism, that the world, all existence, are so

[1] Stern, *Erkenntnistheoretische Probleme der modernen Physik*, Berlin 1952, p. 75.
[2] *Op. cit.*, p. 76.   [3] *Op. cit.*, p. 83.   [4] Fogarasi, *Logik*, p. 349.

constituted that the system of time and space imposes insuperable limitations on man's knowledge and awareness. The reconstruction of past events in nature and particularly in history is subject to uncertainty, because there are periods of time that are not recoverable. Indeed even in the case of events of which we are ourselves witness it is not possible to discover the causes completely or to judge exactly. Because of the passage of time and the immensity of distance perceptibility is comparatively slight and knowledge still less, and neither of them absolute. Even the scientific criterion of repeatability is strictly speaking very seldom realizable and is almost impossible in regard to the vital questions about the origin of our solar system, life and man.

The limitations of knowledge are even narrower with regard to the scientific prediction of future events. Popular scientific literature frequently makes use of a dubious antithesis of scientific prediction and religious prejudice, and confines itself to a few examples, mostly in the inorganic field, deliberately ignoring the numerous cases in everyday experience which continue to defy any scientific prediction. Even A. A. Zhdanov refers somewhat ironically to the difficulties of long-range weather forecasting.[1]

Finally the objective limits of perceptibility are particularly acute in the ability to control phenomena. Indeed even Stalin, as we have seen, refers to geological and analogous processes that are beyond human power to influence. Thus it is clearly impossible to call any earthly-human things or phenomena omnipotent. Even with truth and power combined it would scarcely be possible to speak of omnipotence, for theory and practice show over and over again examples which make it clear that that label is untrue.

Reviewing the philosophical position of materialistic atheism it is clear that at some points it arbitrarily expands or contracts the principles that it has set up. In general it maintains that causality is universal, and then this causality is played off against the miracles of Jesus. On the other hand the same causality when

[1] Zhdanov, *Kritische Bemerkungen*, p. 24.

applied to the question of the origin of the world is narrowed and limited. The leading materialistic philosopher Georg Klaus sets a limit to causality and, obviously in order to avoid the question of the origin of the world, gives priority to the self-movement of matter and internal causes. Self-movement, he says, only exists in the universe as a whole.[1] So also Klohr says, in order to make a creator unnecessary, that the causal relation must not be applied to the world as a whole. The question of the cause of the world is meaningless, because the world is eternal.[2] Another author applies the idea of evolution only to finite material systems, and contests any upward evolution of the finite universe.[3]

From all this it is evident that the philosophical basis of materialistic atheism is to be found neither in experiment nor logic, but in its anti-religious atheistic preconceptions. That is fundamentally why materialistic atheism can hardly do justice to the phenomenon of religion and not at all to the substance of the Gospel. The doctrines of materialistic atheism in their materialistic content are mostly outmoded and out of date. The prophecy of the turn of the century that religion would die out in the face of science, technics and education has not been fulfilled. A look at the modern world, say at Africa or Asia, shows the awakening of heathen nature religions that were supposed to have died out, and a revival of the great religions. Shintoism, Buddhism, Islam and other religions are reviving and for the first time in their long history have found the power to missionize. In the mohammedan world particularly, tradition and progress, religion and nationalism are being combined. These nations are following a new and peculiar path.

In the long run man is not able to do without God, unless he creates ideologies for himself or endows himself with values which he puts in place of God. God or idols ? That is the question facing humanity. This question is of supreme importance for man himself and for the future. It is not possible for man to hold his

---

[1] Klaus, *Jesuiten, Gott, Materie*, p. 307ff.

[2] Klohr, *Naturwissenschaft, Religion und Kirche*, p. 48.

[3] *Deutsche Zeitschrift für Philosophie*, 1958/1/145.

ground in the struggle against God. God will not be shut out from the world, but holds its fate and the life of every individual in his hands. Faith is essential for full humanity; without it a lapse into the purely biological is inevitable, for in God we live and move and have our being.